Cambridge Elements ≡

Elements in Public and Nonprofit Administration
edited by
Andrew Whitford
University of Georgia
Robert Christensen
Brigham Young University

TOPICS IN PUBLIC ADMINISTRATION

Perspectives from Computational Social Sciences and Corpus Linguistics

Richard M. Walker
Lingnan University

Jiasheng Zhang
University of Macau

Yanto Chandra
City University of Hong Kong

CAMBRIDGE
UNIVERSITY PRESS

Shaftesbury Road, Cambridge CB2 8EA, United Kingdom

One Liberty Plaza, 20th Floor, New York, NY 10006, USA

477 Williamstown Road, Port Melbourne, VIC 3207, Australia

314–321, 3rd Floor, Plot 3, Splendor Forum, Jasola District Centre,
New Delhi – 110025, India

103 Penang Road, #05–06/07, Visioncrest Commercial, Singapore 238467

Cambridge University Press is part of Cambridge University Press & Assessment,
a department of the University of Cambridge.

We share the University's mission to contribute to society through the pursuit of
education, learning and research at the highest international levels of excellence.

www.cambridge.org
Information on this title: www.cambridge.org/9781009571982

DOI: 10.1017/9781009378697

First published 2024

A catalogue record for this publication is available from the British Library

ISBN 978-1-009-57198-2 Hardback
ISBN 978-1-009-37871-0 Paperback
ISSN 2515-4303 (online)
ISSN 2515-429X (print)

Topics in Public Administration

Perspectives from Computational Social Sciences and Corpus Linguistics

Elements in Public and Nonprofit Administration

DOI: 10.1017/9781009378697
First published online: November 2024

Richard M. Walker
Lingnan University

Jiasheng Zhang
University of Macau

Yanto Chandra
City University of Hong Kong

Author for correspondence: Richard M. Walker, richardwalker@ln.edu.hk

Abstract: This inductive examination of the topics in the public administration literature using computational social science and corpus linguistics (N = 12,760 articles) reveals a new landscape of public administration topics, changes in topics over time and their distribution. The top ten topics include healthcare, federal government, performance management, environmental regulation, and HRM accounting for just over a third of scholarship between 1991 and 2019. The focal topics identified in individual journals identified similarities with popular topics in the whole corpus – networks, health care, HRM – and less frequently examined topics including gender and diversity and partnerships. Analysis of topics over time shows a substantial flow in topics moving from a country and practice focus to concepts such as governance, networks and citizens. Analysis of the World Bank Governance Indicators indicated that lower scoring countries placed a greater emphasis on structures, while research in countries with higher scores emphasised management and governance.

Keywords: public administration, topics, computational social science, corpus linguistics, time

ISBNs: 9781009571982 (HB), 9781009378710 (PB), 9781009378697 (OC)
ISSNs: 2515-4303 (online), 2515-429X (print)

Contents

1 Introduction

Reviews that take stock of the nature, scope, topics and trajectory of a field of academic enquiry are important for understanding how a discipline has developed over time (George et al. 2023). Reviews often have the purpose of looking back to look forward; that is, they identify what is known to understand what is not known. The discipline of public administration, which draws on political science, economics, law, sociology and so on, is a design science that examines the administration and management of government and the implementation of policies with the aim of understanding how public services can be delivered efficiently, effectively and equitably. Scholars of public administration have sought to unpick and explain the interdisciplinary design science nature of the discipline (Simon 1996) and have examined its topics, origins, maturity and intellectual traditions (Frederickson et al. 2016; Peters and Pierre 2003; Raadschelders 2011). Three approaches have been noteworthy in the literature to date: overarching reviews of the discipline; synthesis and integration reviews; and studies drawing upon bibliometric techniques that provide perspectives on authors, journals and topics.

Public administration scholars have engaged extensively in overarching reviews that synthesise the discipline, including books by leading scholars building on trends in social science and the ways in which knowledge is built. Examples include studies laying out the theoretical foundations of the discipline (Frederickson et al. 2016; Peters and Pierre 2003); examining its theoretical underpinnings and its applied nature (Cox et al. 2016); and exploring tensions within the discipline between administration, politics and law (Rosenbloom et al. 1993), and between administration and management (Ferlie et al. 2005). Others have tackled contemporary questions about globalisation and the modern state (Bohne et al. 2014) and comparative change in public administration practices (Pollitt and Bouckaert 2004). Scholarship on the nature, extent and focus of public administration has also targeted and examined the field in a variety of ways. Some studies have taken a geographically focused target. Walker (2014a) examined the English language literature in Asia; Wu and colleagues (2013) examined mainland China; Li and Zhang (2021) examined studies on China in mainstream public administration journals; and Gulrajani and Moloney (2012) and Raadschelders and Vigoda-Gadot (2015) studied public administration as a global phenomenon.

Some scholars have examined single topics and undertaken systematic reviews and integration studies of topics such as public service motivation (Ritz et al. 2016) or innovation (De Vries et al. 2016; Walker 2014b). Following Perry's (2012) call for more reviews synthesising knowledge in public administration, meta-analyses have become popular in the field. Following Gerrish's (2016) study of performance management, there have been meta-analyses of research on a number of key public administration concepts: bureaucratic representation (Ding et al. 2021; Wang 2024), citizen satisfaction (Zhang, Chen et al. 2022), government performance and citizen trust (Zhang, Li et al. 2022), red tape (George et al. 2021) and strategic management (George et al. 2019). Other studies have examined the institutional framework within which public administration scholarship is located (Van de Walle and van Delft 2015), while still others have drilled down into specific components of these frameworks, for example productivity (Corley and Sabharwal 2010). Bibliographic and bibliometric methods, which use citations and statistical techniques to establish similarity between documents, have been applied to reviews of the theoretical approaches used in public administration (Hattke and Vogel 2023) and to individual topics, such as public organisations (Vogel 2014), public administration and management (Andrews and Esteve 2015), new public management (Curry and Van de Walle 2016) and to understand the diffusion of individual scholarly articles (Chandra and Walker 2018).

Whether the purpose of these reviews was overarching examinations of the discipline or more targeted reviews drawing from the methodological repertoire of bibliometric sciences, all have made important contributions to understanding the nature of knowledge in the field of public administration, its development over time and its future direction, both theoretically and as an applied discipline of the design sciences (Simon 1996). However, the methodologies adopted in reviews published to date can often be characterised as largely (1) deductive, (2) manual, (3) static and (4) overlooking geography. We argue that they are deductive because they have relied on scholars identifying categories for analysis through the development of coding frames, which may take the form of concepts in discursive reviews or variables in a meta-analysis. They have often used manual methodologies because scholars need to code concepts or variables themselves based on their own reading of the research materials, which can result in bias (Ennser-Jedenastik and Meyer 2018; Krippendorf 2004; Norris 1997). They have been static because they are often limited in time span, or do not systematically examine change over time in the concepts and variables of interest. Finally, geography has been typically treated as a dummy variable in meta-analyses, included in focused regional reviews or captured through bibliometric techniques rather than examined across a large corpus.

To address some of these issues, public administration scholars have turned to computational social science and linguistics. Studies in this arena have illustrated the utility of the related methods (Hollibaugh 2019) or examined specific questions, such as the research–practice gap (Walker et al. 2019, 2023), a single journal (Vogel and Hattke 2022) or single concepts, such as red tape (Kaufmann and Haans 2021) or innovation (Pandey et al. 2017). However, and in keeping with the purpose of reviews that take stock of the field of public administration, what is lacking is a systematic review that focuses on what scholars themselves identify as the important topics in public administration through an analysis of their scholarly writing. Our analysis therefore uses intelligent machines. Specifically, we use topic modelling, which is a form of machine learning that uses statistical methods to identify the key topics and words in a corpus. The machines can provide an 'overall picture' that is not influenced by human judgement, which may be biased by keywords or institutions, among other things.

Furthermore, the integration of computational social science and corpus linguistics methodologies offers a valuable opportunity to explicitly explore the dimension of time and understand the evolution, or flow, of topics within the field of public administration. By contrasting studies conducted in early and late periods of corpora, researchers can systematically examine changes in the topics and themes that have emerged over time. This approach allows for a comprehensive analysis of the dynamic nature of the field of public administration, taking into account temporal variations and contextual factors that may influence its development.

In addition to temporal analysis, the inclusion of geography as a factor of investigation can provide further depth and insights into the field of public administration. Geographical considerations allow researchers to examine the distribution of scholarship and how scholars writing in different regions or jurisdictions may shape a field's practices, policies and challenges. By considering spatial dimensions, such as variations in governance structures, regional disparities and the impact of specific contexts, a more comprehensive understanding of public administration can be achieved.

Thus, our investigation adopts inductive computational and linguistic techniques to address the following two research questions.

1. What are the topics in public administration scholarship?
2. Do the topics in public administration vary (1) chronologically and (2) geographically?

In answering question 1, we examine the scholarship in the period 1991–2019 across all journals in our corpus. This allows us to examine the 'stock' of scholarship during this period. Question 2 answers questions about the 'flow' of topics over time and the geographic 'distribution' of topics.

In the following section, we outline our sample, which is the corpus of public administration journals over the 1991–2019 period, methods, procedures and analytical approach. We then proceed to present and discuss our findings. Three sets of analyses are presented. First, we use topic modelling to examine the whole corpus and undertake a 'discipline-level' analysis that identifies the stock of topics in public administration research. We also delve into the dominant topics in individual journals to identify their focus and contrast it with their stated objectives. Second, we look at topic evolution by examining fluctuations and flows in topic weighting (TW) over the 1991–2019 period; we also use corpus linguistics, a discipline that examines patterns of language using statistical methods, to examine keyness – the aboutness or the most common keywords in a text corpus in a probabilistic manner – in the early and late stages of our study period. Third, we delve into geographical variation by conducting a country-level analysis. Here, we use the World Bank Governance Indicators dataset, which covers six governance domains. We highlight geographical variation and distribution of topics by categorising countries as high or low performers and rerun our main analysis using the two subsamples. Finally, we bring together our key findings in the conclusion.

2 Methods and Analytical Procedure

We answer our research questions by applying computational social science and computational linguistics methodologies to a corpus of public administration journal articles. By allowing us to examine an entire large corpus, topic modelling and corpus linguistics can be used to unravel the key content, themes and keyness (i.e., a measure of what keywords that appear the most probabilistically; usually measured using log likelihood ratio (LLR) and p-value) and aboutness (i.e., a generic term to refer to what a document is about, which can be defined using topics such as topic modelling and also using LLR) of the corpus being analysed. We use these techniques to examine the topics in public administration journals and the chronological and geographical changes in topics over the study period. The novelty in our use of these techniques is the application of an inductive method of enquiry that has not been previously used on such an extensive scale.

2.1 The Corpus

The corpus is drawn from journals categorised as public policy and administration journals by Google Scholar Metrics and those in the public administration sections of the Journal Citation Reports published by Clarivate and Scopus' Scimargo Journal Rankings for 2016 (the date we commenced work on this project). The number of journals included in these indexes varies, for example, the Scimargo Journal Rankings is the most comprehensive, including all journals in the other indices and providing a population of over 100 journals, while there are only 47 journals listed in the Journal Citation Reports. Not all journals in these listings focus exclusively on public administration. For example, *Climate Change* and *Policy Sciences* are listed in the public administration category in the Journal Citation Reports, the Scimargo Journal Rankings includes *Administrative Science Quarterly* and *Educational Administration Quarterly*, while Google Scholar Metrics includes *Science and Public Policy*. Some public administration journals are highly specialised by topic and geography, for example *Public Budgeting and Finance*, the *Journal of Homeland Security and Emergency Management* and the *Transylvanian Review of Administrative Sciences*.

To resolve these variations, we implemented a set of decision rules to ensure that our corpus consisted of journals that have the public administration discipline as their core area of enquiry. First, we specified that the primary focus of the journal should be public administration – for example, while Scimargo lists *Administrative Science Quarterly* as the top journal in its public administration category, it publishes a limited number of public administration studies. Its primary focus is organisational theory in different settings. Second, selected journals had to be listed in Google Scholar Metrics, the Journal Citation Reports and the top 50% of Scimargo Journal Rankings (to ensure high levels of rigor of the published articles). The third and fourth criteria were the exclusion of specialist and non-English language journals, respectively.

The application of these decision rules resulted in a corpus consisting of the seventeen journals listed in Table 1, which also shows the year each journal was first listed in the Journal Citation Reports. Journal articles from the 1991–2019 study period were scraped from Web of Science for their metadata, including title, abstract, author information and publication year. The final sample contained 12,760 articles.

Limiting the scope of the study was necessary to ensure its feasibility, and confining the sample to journal articles ensured that the studies met the rigorous standards of scholarly publications. Although this excluded books and reports from governments and international organisations such as the OECD, bias arising from a focus on journal articles has been shown to be small (Rosenthal 1991).

2.2 Topic Modelling

Topic modelling uses a natural language processing technique called Latent Dirichlet Allocation (LDA) to extract topics. Latent Dirichlet Allocation was developed by computer scientists in the mid-2000s and has been extended beyond the field of computer science. The best way to understand topic modelling is the article on probabilistic topic models by Blei (2012). Blei (2012)

Table 1 Journals included in the corpus

Journal title	JCR entry year
Administration & Society (A&S)	1997
American Review of Public Administration (ARPA)	1997
Environment and Planning C: Government and Policy (EPC)	1997
Governance: An International Journal of Policy, Administration and Institutions (Governance)	1997
International Public Management Journal (IPMJ)	2010
International Review of Administrative Sciences (IRAS)	1997
Journal of Public Administration Research and Theory (JPART)	2003
Local Government Studies (LGS)[a]	1999
Policy and Politics (P&P)	1997
Public Administration (PA)	1997
Public Administration and Development (PAD)	1997
Public Administration Review (PAR)	1997
Public Management Review (PMR)[b]	2007
Public Money and Management (PMM)	1997
Public Performance and Management Review (PPMR)	2011
Social Policy and Administration (SPA)	1997

Key:
JCR year = year journal entered the JCR.
[a] Listed in SJR Development and Sociology and Political Science
[b] Was listed in *Marketing* prior to *Public Administration*

showed how using optical character recognition to scan the entire collection of *Science* from 1990 to 2000, a sample containing 17,000 documents and 11 million words, including 20,000 unique terms or words (after excluding stop words and rare words), could produce an LDA output of 100 topics. Advances in this method have explored different classes of topic modelling such as dynamic and correlated topic modelling, structural topic modelling and supervised topic modelling, among others.

Topic modelling is an unsupervised machine learning technique that has gained popularity in other disciplines in the social sciences (e.g., political science, communication studies, management and organisations), although it has only recently been applied to the field of public administration. For example, Chandra et al. (2016), Walker et al. (2019), Li et al. (2022) and were among the earliest researchers to use LDA in public administration to examine cross-sectoral governance. Chandra et al. (2016) used LDA to investigate the patterns in the strategies used by social entrepreneurs to bring about social change. These authors relied on theories from the field of social entrepreneurship to classify the change-making strategies. Walker et al. (2019, 2023) used LDA to conduct a bibliometric study of the evolution of the research–practice gap, a long-standing debate in the field of public administration. Li et al. (2022) used LDA to examine the social media messaging strategies adopted by different levels of the Chinese government during the Covid-19 pandemic. The authors relied on theories from the field of communication to interpret the patterns in the topics that were produced by LDA. Latent Dirichlet Allocation has also been applied to understand patent data (Blei and Lafferty 2007; Kaplan and Vakili 2014).

There are good reasons why topic modelling is useful for social scientists. First, data in the social sciences are often in the form of text. Although some scholars in the social sciences primarily use survey or secondary (closed form) data in their research, many scholars work with textual data. Textual data are interesting because they are unstructured, messy, rich and thick, but can be confusing to read and synthesise, even for well-trained and experienced scholars. This speaks to the importance (and limitations) of human visual acuity in the understanding and detection of 'hidden patterns' in texts. Second, researchers in the social sciences who rely primarily on textual data tend to work with a small body of texts. For example, scholars who primarily work with qualitative data (e.g., in-depth interviews, ethnographic data, newspapers) can only analyse a small number of such texts. It is difficult to imagine how a researcher could manually code and synthesise thousands or hundreds of thousands of pages of texts and come up with reasonable results without being accused of 'cherry picking'. These limitations motivate the use of a computerised tool such as the LDA as a method that can reveal the hidden patterns in a large body of textual data by using iterative cycles of analysis until patterns can be discerned.

To non-experts, LDA can be understood using the analogy of traditional content analysis: the purpose of LDA is nothing more than to synthesise the content of a body of textual data, just like traditional content analysis does. While content analysis can be done manually by human coders and typically qualitatively (e.g., texts such as newspaper articles are coded without the use of predetermined categories), it can also be done quantitatively (e.g., using a coding scheme to assign numerical values to a sample of texts treated as data and then conducting statistical analysis of these numerical values). To those who are more conversant with general linear models in frequentist statistics, LDA can be seen as another data reduction method similar to exploratory factor analysis (EFA). However, while EFA requires close-ended data (e.g., 1–5 or metric scales), LDA is applied to textual data. However, both methods have the same purpose: to reduce the dimensions to a manageable number so that the results can be easily interpreted, more parsimoniously. There are some trade-offs in how to decide which outputs to use. Latent Dirichlet Allocation is more positivistic (versus interpretative) in its epistemology, from the perspective of the philosophy of science.

Latent Dirichlet Allocation works by making inferences from observed meanings (or 'topics') in a large body of textual data, for example books, journal articles, newspaper articles, magazines or patent data (Blei 2012; Blei and Jordan 2003). This means that LDA is probabilistic in nature and thus is not an absolute or deterministic method with closed-form mathematical equations as outputs. (Although the equations driving the algorithms in LDA in Python or R programming languages are nothing short of fantastic mathematical equations.) The probabilistic nature of LDA also means that for the LDA method to work effectively, it requires human intervention – humans make decisions on how many topics to produce, examine, interpret and provide labels to the topic outputs and reiterate the process until the best outputs are achieved. The word 'best' here usually means that the topics are easy to discern, are clearly differentiated and can be ranked according to their importance (e.g., by topic weight, semantic coherence, exclusivity).

Latent Dirichlet Allocation is therefore essentially a collection of computer algorithms. Technically, LDA assumes that each document (e.g., a Harry Potter novel) contains a variety of topics, but that the topics are usually unobservable or latent (e.g., Harry had a bad childhood is one topic; Harry, Ron and Hermione's relationship is another topic), and these topics stand between (i.e., do not appear vividly to readers because they are 'hidden' in an ocean of words) the documents and terms (Blei 2012; Paul and Dredze 2014; Tirunillai and Tellis 2014). This essentially means that topics are meso-level information that are not easily spotted by human readers, while the actual words (or terms) and documents are the highly observable micro and macro levels of texts, respectively.

By laying out the terms (or observable 'micro' level data listed in rows) that exist in a set of documents (or observable 'macro' level data listed in columns) in a dataset (a matrix that can be produced using any computational tools), LDA probabilistically infers what topics (or 'meso' level information) exist in the documents (Chandra et al. 2016; Landauer et al. 2013). Far from being a straightforward, one-way inference, LDA works iteratively by first making assumptions about the relationships among terms and the documents and then making inferences from the posterior expectation or posterior inference problem (that is, the p (topics, proportions, assignments | documents)). Specifically, it assigns topics and proportions of topics to words and documents where (i) each topic is associated with a distribution of different words, (ii) each document contains a mixture of various topics and (iii) each word is drawn from one of the topics (see Blei 2012). Latent Dirichlet Allocation achieves its optimal results using trade-off rules. That is, for each document, LDA allocates the words or terms to as few topics as possible (e.g., Document 1 is 95% Topic A, 3% Topic B and 1% Topic C, whereas Document 2 is 20% Topic A and 80% Topic B). For each topic, it assigns a high probability to as few terms as possible (e.g., two common topics in news stories are 'inflation' and 'politics' and the most common terms associated with inflation might be 'price', 'high', 'shortage' and 'war', while the words associated with the politics topic might be 'NATO', 'Russia', 'Ukraine' and 'war'; note that the term 'war' is common in both topics). Achieving a high probability that a term represents a certain topic and reducing the number of terms used in the analysis are contradictory goals – requiring a trade-off – because the former requires assigning all of the words in a document to a few topics, while the latter requires (grouping) multiple words to have a high probability of being used in a single topic. The result of this trade-off is the identification of tightly co-occurring words. Accordingly, LDA is a general tool rather than a tool for a specific purpose. Humans can observe the documents and the terms, but the hidden structures, which are the topics, are not visible to human reader because of the vast number of words, and LDA uses algorithms to infer the topics and make them visible based on the distribution of words in the documents.

Accordingly, LDA uses the distribution of terms over documents (or a 'document–term matrix') to probabilistically estimate term–topic relationships (or a 'term–topic' matrix) and document–topic relationships (or a 'document–term matrix'). In other words, LDA uses a number of 'terms' (e.g., sushi, burger, curry; summer, airline, hotel) to classify and define 'topics' (e.g., 'food', 'holiday'); each document can be associated with several topics (e.g., food, Japan, well-being), but each document has a primary topic represented by the highest topic–document probability with lower probabilities for other topics.

Among the most popular techniques for implementing LDA is the topicmodels package for the R programming language (Hornik and Grün 2011). Other popular R packages for topic modelling include the tm package (Feinerer 2015), which is often used to pre-process and convert the corpus to create a document–term matrix. Other packages include dplyr (for unstructured data manipulation), quanteda (a general tool for natural language processing, including data manipulation and sentiment analysis) and ggplot2 (for data visualisation). One can also perform LDA using other programming languages such as Python with the help of pyLDAvis, Gensim or nltk pandas.

The first step in our LDA methodology was to capture journal names and author information (e.g., names, country of origin, department and university affiliation). We primarily relied on 'title + abstract' as the main data for topic modelling analysis. We used the topicmodels package in R to estimate and identify an initial list of topics (e.g., representative bureaucracy, collaboration, performance management) in the sample corpus of journal articles. We followed the best practices for LDA (e.g., Chandra et al. 2016; Quinn et al. 2010) by involving human experts who read and interpreted the LDA topic outputs and provided names for each topic, that is, 'topic labels' (e.g., the group of terms 'learning, improvement and measurement' was labelled the 'performance management' topic). Any obviously overlapping topics were merged (relying on expert readers' consensus) to ensure a more meaningful analysis. As LDA is a probabilistic tool for discovery (i.e., a bottom-up approach), we did not predetermine the number of topics at the outset but rather worked with the topics interactively, interpreting them, labelling them and then narrowing them down to a manageable number of topics.

Following the identification of key topics, we calculated the 'total topic weight' for each topic identified in the corpus and assigned a primary topic to each journal article. The total topic weight was a proxy for the relative popularity of a topic. The total topic weight was the dependent variable. This analysis was undertaken on the whole corpus and then separately for each journal.

2.2.1 Naming the Topics: Expert Panel

The inductive methodology of topic modelling provided keywords for each identified topic, but did not provide topic names: human input was required to name the topics. Given that human input into the process of naming topics can be somewhat subjective, an expert panel was established. Experts were selected to reflect the geographical representation of the corpus: the Americas, Asia-Pacific and Europe. Eleven experts agreed to take part in the survey, with ten completing the study.

Using Delphi panel techniques, we conducted two rounds of a survey to seek consensus on topic names. Panel recruitment took place in March 2022, with Round 1 conducted through April and early May and Round 2 from late May to early June 2022. In Round 1, expert panel members were sent an MSWord file containing the fifty sets of the top five terms generated by the LDA analysis for each unnamed topic and asked to provide a name for each topic based on the terms included in each set. Following responses from panel members, the authors implemented two decision rules to identify 'common' topic names: (1) we parsimoniously sought to have topic names of no more than two words and (2) majority voting. This provided a first draft of the topic names. In Round 2, an MSExcel file was sent to the experts. In this file, we anonymously listed the names proposed by the members of the expert panel in Round 1, and the topic name proposed by the authors. In the final column of the Excel file, the experts were asked to indicate their support for the proposed name or to offer an alternative. Ten experts responded to the second round of the survey. The final topic names are presented in Section 3. There was strong consensus on the proposed names: there was 100% support for twenty-four of the topic names, 90% support for sixteen, 80% for six and 70% for four of the topic names. We did not repeat this process for the identification of topics in each of the seventeen journals in our corpus; we did it ourselves without using the expert panel.

2.3 Corpus Linguistics

We complemented the topic analysis with computational linguistics, or corpus linguistics, which allowed us to further analyse the characteristics of the corpus. Corpus linguistics is a discipline that examines patterns of language using statistical methods where a target corpus is compared with a reference corpus; it is also a methodology of choice of scholars in various disciplines from political science, marketing, digital humanities to terrorism and media studies. Using WordSmith, a popular corpus linguistics software, we studied the keyness or aboutness of the corpus by calculating the LLR of time at the discipline and journal levels by dividing the sample into early and late periods and comparing the topic distribution in the two subsamples. Here, we first explain corpus linguistics.

Corpus linguistics is a method for analysing the language in large bodies of text (Chandra 2016a, b; Rayson 2008). A body of text is known as a corpus in the singular and corpora in the plural. In essence, corpus linguistics is a methodology for analysing language data in either spoken or written form (although most spoken data are transcribed into text form for corpus linguistics analysis) using corpus linguistics software (Rayson 2008). Corpus linguistics has a qualitative heritage; it existed in manual form for decades prior to the age of computerisation and this form continues to be used for studies with small samples (Chandra and Shang 2019) that are analysed by 'hand and by eye' (McEnery and Hardie 2012, p. 3). However, in today's digital age, scholars who conduct analysis of large corpora (Perren and Sapsed 2013) usually perform the analysis using sophisticated corpus linguistics machines. However, the affordance of corpus linguistics has been greatly enhanced by the digitisation of text, the public availability of materials on the Internet (Bennett 2015) and the rise of modern computational tools that support corpus linguistics analysis such as WordSmith, BNCWeb, AntConc and the open-source package in R (Gries 2016). These data and technologies are external enablers that allow researchers to manipulate and process corpora make up of millions and potentially billions of words, ushering in an era of digital humanities or digital social sciences. Accordingly, advances in computing technologies have sparked a 'quantitative turn' in corpus linguistics.

The texts used in corpus linguistics are usually gathered using systematic sampling techniques focused on a specific research question, literature or theory (and at times on certain hypotheses), organised into datasets (the corpora). These are then explored or validated quantitatively and qualitatively (McEnery and Hardie 2012). The data can also be drawn from a census for some research question (e.g., studying how words co-occur or the aboutness of all articles published in *Nature* or *Science*). The findings in corpus linguistics are presented in a variety of formats, including tables that show the ratios of the frequencies of the focal objects in the target corpus against a reference corpus; mathematical formulae (e.g., measures of association of words such as mutual information); strings of words (e.g., *n*-gram analysis); statistical figures (e.g., LLR, chi-square statistics of the chance of occurrence of words); in visual representations (e.g., semantic category analysis showing categories of words with different probabilities of occurrence using larger or smaller font size for ease of viewing) and concordance analysis (showing a keyword and one word to the left and one word to the right of a keyword of interest, and agglomerative clustering of words, and analysing them qualitatively to discover themes). No single study uses all of these techniques; the selection depends on the researchers' objectives and research questions.

Researchers interested in the association of a particular word (e.g., the corpus linguistics study of red tape by Kaufmann and Haans (2021)) have focused on bi-gram analysis. While unigram is essentially a single word, such as 'coffee', 'football' or 'email', bi-gram, or lexical bundle, means two words that are frequently used together, such as 'drink coffee' or 'play football' or 'send emails'. But bi-gram can also take different forms. For example, if one takes all published papers on Covid-19 and analyses their titles, the bi-grams could include 'Covid-19 and', 'Covid-19 pandemic', 'of Covid-19', 'the Covid-19'; these can be used to understand the language patterns use but also the attention of researchers to the topic. When we pair three words together as a bundle, this is called tri-gram (e.g., 'the Covid-19 pandemic', 'Covid-19 vaccination is' and 'Covid-19 caused many'); and when four words are paired together, this refers to four-gram (e.g., 'the Covid-19 pandemic has', 'Covid-19 vaccination is administered' and 'Covid-19 caused many deaths'). The list can go on into what we call *n*-gram. Thus, *n*-gram is a short phrase of a variety of word pairs that are being analysed. *N*-gram is useful because researchers are interested in understanding how language producers (e.g., policymakers, learners, terrorists, surgeons and politicians) deploy language in a particular area.

Bi-grams are parsimonious and are useful when a researcher is interested in understanding how policymakers deploy language in a particular policy area. To understand language use – and how it fits into the arena of public administration – researchers may analyse the parliamentary (or congressional) discourse, media discourse or campaign language used by certain policymakers. Scholars have applied corpus linguistics to an archival corpus of parliamentary records in Westminster states to examine how they differ across the United Kingdom, Canada, Singapore and Vanuatu or to a specialised but small corpus from a particular organisation (Perren and Sapsed 2013; Rheault and Cochrane 2020). For example, Perren and Sapsed (2013) analysed British parliamentary records in relation to innovation policy over a forty-five-year period and revealed that the term 'innovation' has gradually gained political importance, both in absolute numbers (i.e., frequency of use) and qualitatively, as shown by its position within political discourse (and by extension government policy and action). As another example, Chandra (2016a) used corpus linguistics to understand the language of change-making used by social entrepreneurs (defined as individuals who combine business and nonprofit logics to tackle societal problems such as poverty, discrimination or climate change). Chandra performed collocations (bi-gram analysis) on a social enterprise taxi that serves disabled and elderly passengers using a small, specialised corpus, and then selected several keywords and drilled deeper using concordance analysis. He showed that corpus linguistics can serve as a tool to assist scholars to build and/or test theories. For example, he found that 'wheelchair' collocates with 'user', 'bound', 'accessible' and 'friendly'; and 'disabled' collocates with 'persons', 'permanently', 'carry' and 'transportation'; while 'elderly' collocates with 'homes', 'commission' and 'wheelchair'. These allow the researcher to understand how such terms are used by the social entrepreneur of interest (in the interviews) and media coverage about the social enterprise concerned.

Corpus linguistics underlines the idea that 'words matter' (Perren and Sapsed 2013, p. 1726) in our understanding of and practice in the social world, particularly for public administration. The field of public administration is inherently linguistic; it is expressed and performed through language. This understanding means that public administration scholarship should analyse the 'talk and text' (Prior et al. 2012, p. 272) of public administrators as well as the works of public administration scholars. This summarises succinctly the main objectives of corpus linguistics: to complement, triangulate and provide empirical rigor to the conventional positivist mode of research (e.g., surveys, experiments) and constructivist field discourse analysis (Fairclough 2013). Corpus linguistics offers a hybrid method associated with both positivism and constructionism.

Far from being dominated by a single field, corpus linguistics is interdisciplinary in its application. Researchers have used corpus linguistics to study linguistics, communication, law, sociology and management studies (O'Reilly and Reed 2011), as well as political science (L'Hôte 2010), public health (Prior et al. 2012) and medical science (Pastrana et al. 2008). Researchers have used corpus linguistics techniques to examine questions related to actors (government and non-government, business and nonprofit), objects (public administration, service delivery and cross-sectoral partnerships) and organisations (e.g., social enterprises; Chandra 2016a; Parkinson and Howorth 2008). However, corpus linguistics remains rarely used in public administration. (An exception is Kaufmann and Haans' study (2021) of red tape.)

Viewing corpus linguistics (Baker and McEnery 2005; Chandra 2016a, 2016b; Rayson 2008) as a natural complement to topic modelling analysis, we used it in combination with our LDA analyses. We used the WordSmith tool (Scott 2008) to perform corpus linguistics analysis and to pre-process the corpus into a suitable format for analysis. We divided the corpus into several sub-corpora (e.g., early versus late periods) and focused on the following techniques. First, we examined the keyness (the aboutness) of the corpus by calculating the LLR of a target corpus or sub-corpus (e.g., the early period) relative to a reference sub-corpus (e.g., late period). This produced a list of terms or words with high to low LLRs and their p-values across the target and reference corpus.

2.4 Geography of the Topics in Public Administration

To undertake a comparative analysis of topics across countries/regions, we grouped the topics according to the country/region the first/corresponding author was located in for each article. This approach may face limitations such as the first or corresponding authors being based in a different country than those examined in the article. However, this variable does capture the geography of scholarship in public administration by identifying the country of the university/institution showing leadership and the generation of knowledge in this field.

To provide a framework to understand the geography of scholarship, we used the World Bank Governance Indicators. These indicators evaluate various dimensions of governance across 213 countries and territories for the 1996–2020 period. We categorised the countries/regions in our sample using these indicators. The time period for the World Bank Governance Indicators overlaps with our sample period, permitting analysis. Six dimensions of governance are included in the index, and each dimension is measured on a scale from −2.5 to +2.5, with higher values indicating better governance. While the indicators may have their inherent biases or limitations and are subject to interpretation and criticism, they provide a valuable tool for understanding governance trends and informing policy discussions worldwide. The indicators are as follows.

- Voice and accountability: The extent to which citizens can participate in the selection of their government, freedom of expression and the existence of free media.
- Political stability and absence of violence: The likelihood of political instability, violence or terrorism within a country.
- Government effectiveness: The quality of public services, the competence of civil servants and the government's capacity to implement policies effectively.
- Rule of law: The extent to which the government and its agents operate within a framework of laws and regulations, and the degree to which the judiciary is independent and impartial.
- Regulatory quality: The ability of the government to formulate and implement sound policies and regulations that promote private sector development and protect the public interest.
- Control of corruption: The presence of corruption in the public sector and the effectiveness of anticorruption efforts.

Our method had two steps. First, the three authors independently evaluated the conceptual overlap between the fifty public administration topics identified in the LDA analysis and the governance indicators and assigned each topic to one governance indicator. In the first round, inter-coder reliability (Krippendorff's alpha) was 0.63. During the second round, we conducted extensive discussions and reached on an agreement on the topic assignments. The results of this analysis are presented in Section 5.

Second, to measure geographic differences, each country/territory was given a percentile governance rank based on the World Bank Governance Indicators scheme, ranging from 0 (lowest) to 100 (highest). We averaged the percentile rank data from 1996 to 2020 and calculated the score for each governance dimension. We further divided the samples into low and high score subsamples, with 80 as the cut-off value for the high score subsample. The rationale was based on the distribution of the data: the articles in our sample had an average score of 80–90 on the six indicators with a standard deviation of approximately 10. Therefore, if a country/territory has a score below 80, for example, on control of corruption, it means that the country has a relatively poor performance on corruption control, while countries/regions scoring above 80 have relatively better performance.

To compare the extent to which each governance indicator was examined in the scholarship in our corpus, we summed the number of documents that considered the topics associated with each governance category and calculated that category's prominence. For example, topics related to performance management, human resource management (HRM), networks, local government and so on were grouped into the government effectiveness category, and the number of documents focused on all of these topics was used to calculate the prominence of governance effectiveness in the public administration literature. A number of our topics did not align with any World Bank Governance Indicator, and we categorised these topics as 'unknown'.

3 Topics in Public Administration

3.1 Topics in the Corpus of Public Administration Journals

Table 2 presents the findings of our topic modelling analysis. It provides information on the topic rank (column 1), which was derived from the topic weight (column 5) and the number of articles associated with the topic (column 4). The topic names, developed by the expert panel, are given in column 2, and column 6 provides the top five terms for each topic generated by the topic modelling analysis. Figure 1 provides a visual depiction of the stock of topics in public administration between 1991 and 2019.

The highest ranked topic was health care, which accounted for 4.1% of all scholarships in our corpus of public administration journals. In contrast, training, which ranked as the fiftieth most common topic, accounted for just under 1% of the scholarship over the 1991–2019 period. The top five topics – health care, federal government, performance management, environmental regulation and HRM – accounted for just under a fifth (17.9%) of academic writing, while the bottom five – evaluation, risk management, conflict management, procedural justice and training – accounted for just over a twentieth (5.35%) of the scholarship. The top ten topics captured over one-third (34.6%) of all public administration scholarships. The bottom ten topics (ranks 41–50) accounted for just over a tenth (11.7%) of the scholarship.

The discipline of public administration is a design science that examines the administration and management of government and the implementation of policies to understand how public services can be delivered efficiently, effectively and equitably. Our results show, as might be expected, that the topics capture this focus, but with varying weights.

Some twenty topics examined questions of administration and management, accounting for 40.4% of all topics. Three of these topics were among the top ten topics: performance management (TW = 3.8%), HRM (TW = 3.0%) and networks (TW = 3.0%). Three other topics were associated with interorganisational management: networks (TW = 3.0%), collaboration (TW = 2.6%) and partnerships (TW = 2.2%). They were characterised by terms associated with

Table 2 The topics in public administration

Topic rank	Topic name	% expert agreement	N	Topic weight	Top five terms				
1	Health care	90	524	0.04106583	health	care	nhs	healthcare	older
2	Federal government	100	499	0.03910658	federal	executive	commission	legislative	office
3	Performance management	100	488	0.03824451	performance	learning	measurement	indicators	improvement
4	Environmental regulation	100	392	0.03072100	environmental	regulatory	regulation	sustainability	water
5	HRM	90	383	0.03001567	employees	satisfaction	job	perceptions	commitment
6	Networks	100	381	0.02985893	network	networks	trust	coordination	informal
7	Citizen participation	100	350	0.02742947	participation	citizen	involvement	democracy	legitimacy
8	Transparency	100	343	0.02688088	transparency	rules	law	legal	standards
9	Science policy	100	342	0.02680251	science	fields	modern	scientific	themes
10	Local government	90	326	0.02554859	municipalities	municipal	politicians	elected	party
11	Welfare regimes	90	314	0.02460815	welfare	china	regime	regimes	chinese
12	Privatization	100	302	0.02366771	business	firms	privatization	enterprises	companies
13	Culture and values	90	292	0.02288401	values	culture	cultural	npm	dutch
14	Collaboration	90	288	0.02257053	collaborative	collaboration	police	staff	bureaucrats
15	Partnerships	100	286	0.02241379	partnerships	project	projects	partnership	cooperation
16	Contracting	90	283	0.02217868	contracting	competition	cost	contract	providers
17	Representative bureaucracy	100	280	0.02194357	bureaucratic	bureaucracy	diversity	accounting	representation

Table 2 (cont.)

Topic rank	Topic name	% expert agreement	N	Topic weight			Top five terms		
18	Labour/employment policy	90	275	0.02155172	employment	labour	workers	labor	unemployment
19	Strategic planning	100	262	0.02053292	planning	strategic	rural	tools	spatial
20	E-government	100	261	0.02045455	adoption	technology	media	communication	egovernment
21	Gender and diversity	80	259	0.02029781	innovation	women	gender	innovations	career
22	Public finance	90	257	0.02014107	tax	revenue	pension	finance	schemes
23	Finance/budgeting	90	256	0.02006270	fiscal	budget	intergovernmental	budgeting	balance
24	Development aid	90	252	0.01974922	south	assistance	aid	africa	ngos
25	Nonprofits	90	238	0.01865204	nonprofit	funding	board	equity	nonprofits
26	Senior civil servants	70	236	0.01849530	servants	climate	departments	senior	australia
27	Emergency management	100	234	0.01833856	complexity	failure	task	emergency	events
28	Neoliberal paradigm	90	222	0.01739812	crisis	radical	paradigm	crises	neoliberal
29	PSM and red tape	100	221	0.01731975	knowledge	psm	motivation	red	tape
30	Security	90	219	0.01716301	security	meaning	coalition	beliefs	discourses
31	Education	70	211	0.01653605	school	schools	students	university	universities
32	Spending	80	210	0.01645768	spending	size	expenditure	per	funds
33	Europe	80	208	0.01630094	europe	domestic	transition	transfer	germany
34	Accountability	100	205	0.01606583	accountability	expectations	responsiveness	logic	agents
35	Regional governance	100	203	0.01590909	regional	regions	region	metropolitan	multilevel
36	Economic policy	100	197	0.01543887	capital	investment	industrial	economies	scale

#	Term							
37	Urban governance	90	196	0.01536050	urban	corruption	pay	collective	regeneration
38	Local decentralization	70	188	0.01473354	decentralization	city	cities	jurisdictions	transport
39	Leadership	100	187	0.01465517	leadership	leaders	skills	style	transformational
40	Inequality	90	186	0.01457680	poverty	income	exclusion	inequality	inclusion
41	Multilevel governance	80	178	0.01394984	integration	integrated	governing	devolution	wales
42	Housing	70	171	0.01340125	housing	behaviour	special	britain	section
43	Family policy	100	168	0.01316614	administrators	family	identity	children	families
44	User choice	100	167	0.01308777	choice	Users	preferences	rational	safety
45	Organizational autonomy	80	152	0.01191223	autonomy	organisations	voluntary	bodies	reporting
46	Evaluation	100	149	0.01167712	evaluation	criteria	quantitative	techniques	evaluations
47	Risk management	100	140	0.01097179	risk	incentives	risks	uncertainty	experiment
48	Conflict management	100	131	0.01026646	conflict	conflicts	tensions	consensus	competing
49	Procedural justice	100	126	0.00987461	justice	explanations	century	canada	procedural
50	Training	80	122	0.00956113	training	initiative	ireland	northern	intervention

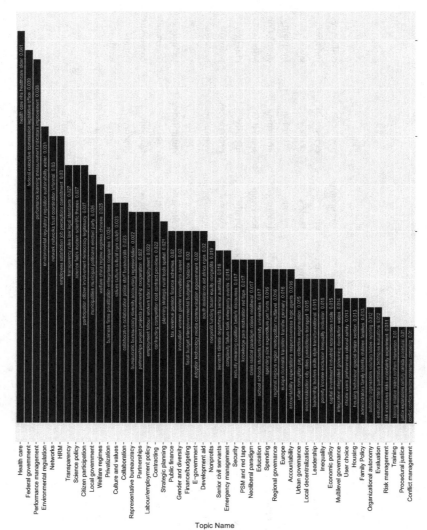

Figure 1 The topics in public administration

management rather than structures, such as coordination, cooperation and projects. Three of the twenty topics were dedicated to government funding and its expenditure: public finance (TW = 2.0%), financing/budgeting (TW = 2.0%) and spending (TW = 1.6%). A number of topics were also associated with individual behaviour in bureaucracies, such as HRM (TW = 3.0%), senior civil servants (TW = 1.8%) and leadership (TW = 1.5%). Some individual management practices were also examined, including strategic planning (TW = 2.1%) and e-government (TW = 2.0%). This suggests that much of the scholarship in public administration is concerned with understanding the processes of management and administration within governments.

Looking first at the topics related to policy, our modelling identified eleven topics, of which ten focused on explicit policy areas and the remaining topic examined how policies are assessed, with a topic weight (TW) of 21.4%. The ten explicit policy topics were heath care (TW = 4.1%), environmental regulation (TW = 3.1%), science policy (TW = 2.7%), labour/employment policy (TW = 2.2%), development aid (TW = 2.0%), education (TW = 1.7%), economic policy (TW = 1.5%), inequality (TW = 1.5%), housing (TW = 1.3%) and family policy (TW = 1.3%). However, one limitation of topic modelling we conducted is that we were not able to directly correlate topics with published journal articles because the technique decomposes the articles into a topic matrix of words. We were thus not able to determine if these studies examined the efficiency, effectiveness and equity of policy or the processes of administration and management in these policy contexts. One example of this would be the extensive work of Kenneth J. Meier and Laurence J. O'Toole Jr. and colleagues, who developed a dataset of management and performance in the field of education policy. They have published on topics in managerial networking, personnel stability and management and their impact on organisational performance (Meier and O'Toole 2003a, 2003b), and their work has considered questions of the effectiveness and equity of public service delivery in school settings, thereby combining questions of management and policy consequences. One topic in the policy category, evaluation (TW = 1.2%), examined the assessment of policies. This suggests that just over a fifth of the scholarship in the corpus we examined was dedicated to questions of policy implementation.

Ten of the fifty topics were associated with the structures and processes of governance associated with structures, giving this area a TW of 18.7%. This included two of the top ten ranked topics, federal government (TW = 3.9%) and local government (TW = 2.6%), and the governance topics related to regional governance (TW = 1.6%), local decentralisation (TW = 1.5%) and multilevel governance (TW = 1.4%). Two of the structure topics also captured scholarship on the nonprofit sector – nonprofits (TW = 1.9%) and organisational autonomy

(TW = 1.2%) – which were characterised by the topic terms voluntary, organisations and bodies. Two topics related to broad structural questions about the best arrangements for delivering public services were privatisation (TW = 2.4%) and contracting (TW = 2.2%), which were characterised by terms such as competition, firms and providers.

Under the broad category of accountability (TW = 5.6%), there were three topics: accountability (TW = 1.6%), which was characterised by the term responsiveness; citizen participation (TW = 2.7%); and user choice (TW = 1.3%). Based on topic names and terms, only two topics could be directly associated with more conceptual work in the discipline. These related to welfare regimes (TW = 2.5%) and the neoliberal paradigm (TW = 1.7%). As with our analysis of topics and their broad categories, the technique of topic modelling did not allow us to identify the specific articles associated with these topics and to fully understand if they are more conceptually or empirically orientated. However, at face value, the balance of the topics was associated with applied research.

In contrast, one topic examined the legal dimension of public administration, procedural justice (TW = 1.0%), while the topic of transparency (TW = 2.7%) drew on terms such as law, legal and rules and standards, suggesting that it had some association with the legal aspects of public administration. One topic had an explicit geographical title and focused on Europe (TW = 1.6%).

In summary, when we examined the stock of scholarship in public administration journals between 1991 and 2019, we found that (1) around 40% of all topics examined broad questions of administration and management, (2) just over a fifth topics related to policy, (3) just under a fifth related to questions of the structures and processes of governance and (4) a twentieth to accountability.

3.2 Topics in Individual Journals

We conducted a separate topic modelling analysis for each journal and identified thirty-five topics for each journal, rather than the fifty for the topics in the discipline because the corpora were smaller. To make inter-journal comparison easier, we focused on the top ten topics for each journal. These analyses had two purposes. First, we sought to examine the extent to which the topics identified in each journal's sample of published articles were consistent with the journal's stated aims (quotations below are taken from the website of each journal and the sources are included in the references section). Second, we compared each journal's top ten topics with the topics in the whole corpus, seeking to determine within the stock of topics in all journals what were common across the stock of topics within journals and to what extent terms were shared in the common topics. (See the topic labels in Table 2 and Figure 1.)

Administration & Society seeks to further the 'understanding of public and human service organizations, their administrative processes, and their effect on society'. Many of its top ten topics (see Table 3), including health care, education, welfare, citizen participation and gender and diversity, correspond with the journal's main aim. The journal is particularly interested in '(1) studies that analyze the effects of the introduction of administrative strategies, programs, change interventions, and training; and (2) studies of intergroup, interorganizational, and organization-environment relationships and policy processes'. This specific focus is reflected in several of the identified topics, such as civil servant, nonprofits, new public management (NPM), HRM and governance outcomes.

Most of the journal's top ten topics are consistent with the whole corpus. Two exceptions are NPM and governance outcomes, suggesting that the journal pays special attention to the impact of NPM reforms and governance outcomes. A comparison of the specific terms in the topics shared between the journal and the whole corpus suggests that the focuses are different. For example, in the education topic, the representative terms in the whole corpus are schools, universities and students, whereas those in *A&S* are federal programmes, schools and goals.

American Review of Public Administration focuses on 'public administration broadly defined, publishing scholarship on all aspects of the field, including such areas as organization and management studies, program and performance evaluation, and budgeting and financial management, network governance, public involvement, and public service motivation'. The top ten topics are mostly consistent with the journal's scope, especially networks, partnerships, HRM, public service motivation (PSM), strategic management and representative bureaucracy (see Table 4). A comparison of the specific terms of the topics shared by the journal and the whole corpus reveals some nuances. For example, for the strategic planning topic, representative terms in the whole corpus are rural, tools and spatial – terms that seem to suggest a relationship with urban planning, whereas in *ARPA* the terms include values, conflict and formal – terms that are more central to strategic planning in public administration.

Environment Planning C: Politics and Space seeks to 'advance debates on the spatialization of politics and the politicization of spatial relations'. In other words, it focuses on the processes that make spatial and environmental issues politically relevant or contested. Among the top ten topics (see Table 5), climate change, energy, innovation and regional governance are closely related to the journal's aims. The fact that the journal has four unique topics, including climate change, energy, innovation and entrepreneurship, indicates that it is

Table 3 Top ten topics in *Administration & Society*

Topic ID	Topic weight	Number	Top five terms				
Gender and diversity	0.0446	39	women	officials	gender	representation	professional
Civil servant	0.0400	35	civil	law	constitutional	servants	modern
Citizen participation	0.0400	35	citizens	participation	citizen	transparency	relationship
Nonprofits	0.0389	34	institutional	nonprofit	activities	nonprofits	identify
NPM	0.0389	34	implementation	npm	financial	reforms	crisis
Governance outcomes	0.0366	32	governance	outcomes	cultural	international	design
Health care	0.0366	32	managers	care	health	strategic	strategies
Education	0.0355	31	programs	federal	program	schools	goal
Welfare	0.0355	31	change	culture	welfare	problem	staff
HRM	0.0355	31	performance	relationship	employees	attitudes	job

Table 4 Top ten topics in *American Review of Public Administration*

Topic ID	Topic weight	Number of documents	Top five terms				
HRM	0.0628	43	job	satisfaction	employee	turnover	workers
Networks	0.0540	37	network	networks	coordination	disaster	ties
PSM	0.0423	29	psm	attitudes	whistleblowing	direct	fit
Strategic planning	0.0423	29	values	planning	strategic	conflict	formal
E-government	0.0423	29	adoption	transparency	e-government	innovation	online
Nonprofits	0.0409	28	nonprofit	funding	advocacy	income	entrepreneurship
Partnership	0.0409	28	collaborative	collaboration	partnerships	stakeholder	partnership
Power balance	0.0394	27	law	legislative	constitutional	court	powers
Representative bureaucracy	0.0365	25	representation	bureaucrats	bureaucracy	discretion	active
Local government	0.0365	25	cities	city	municipal	manager	mayors

Table 5 Top ten topics in *Environment and Planning C: Government and Policy*

Topic ID	Topic weight	Number of documents	Top five terms				
Finance and budgeting	0.0500	61	fiscal	decentralization	expenditure	revenue	intergovernmental
Climate change	0.0492	60	climate	adaptation	leadership	migration	frame
Energy	0.0451	55	energy	emissions	carbon	consumption	targets
Health care	0.0435	53	health	decentralisation	devolution	welfare	care
Public finance	0.0410	50	tax	income	incentives	taxation	rates
Privatization	0.0394	48	enterprise	ethnic	training	assistance	advice
Innovation	0.0394	48	innovation	learning	universities	collaborative	agreements
Entrepreneurship	0.0353	43	entrepreneurship	entrepreneurs	entrepreneurial	concentration	portfolio
Partnerships	0.0345	42	partnerships	regeneration	partnership	members	partners
Regional governance	0.0312	38	municipalities	metropolitan	size	waste	conflicts

a specialised journal focusing on these topics. However, the other topics, such as finance and budgeting, health care, public finance, privatisation and partnerships, seem somewhat unrelated to the relationship between political and spatial issues and may reflect the journal's prior title, which included the subtitle *Government and Policy* rather than *Politics and Space*.

If we compare the terms in the topics shared between the whole corpus and this journal, we can identify some nuances. For example, in the public finance topic, while both corpora focus on taxes, the whole corpus focuses more on pensions and revenue, whereas *EPC* focuses more on incentives, rates and taxation – terms related to different ways to promote business development.

Governance provides a forum for 'the theoretical and practical discussion of executive politics, public policy, administration, and the organization of the state'. Several of the top ten topics, such as delegation, corruption, transparency, supranational governance and multilevel governance, speak perfectly to the journal's focus on executive politics and the organisation of the state (see Table 6). Topics related to finance and budgeting, service provision, economic policy and gender and diversity correspond to the journal's interest in public policy and administration. The remaining topic seems to be related to organisational adaptation in China, demonstrating the journal's international and comparative approach.

Comparisons of the terms in the topics shared by the whole corpus and this journal reveal some differences. For example, for the economic policy topic, the whole corpus focuses on investment, economies and scale, whereas *Governance* focuses on crisis, the IMF and water – terms that seem to reflect how different governing bodies like the IMF respond to crisis, reflecting the journal's narrow focus within economic policy.

The *International Public Management Journal* features research on 'public management and government reform, comparative public administration, organizational theory, and organizational behavior'. Several of the topics identified in the analysis, such as HRM, public finance, networks, contracting and red tape, are related to broad public management and government reform issues (see Table 7). There are also articles examining turnover, PSM and discretion, which are part of the organisational behaviour literature. The journal seems to focus on public management issues, such as coproduction, in the health and education fields.

Comparisons of the terms used to denote topics in the whole corpus versus this journal reveal nuanced differences. For example, for the contracting topic, the terms used in the whole sample (competition, cost, providers) primarily relate to the structural aspects and dynamics of the contracting process, whereas the terms related to this topic in the journal's corpus (strategic, perceived, fiscal,

Table 6 Top ten topics in *Governance: An International Journal of Policy, Administration and Institutions*

Topic ID	Topic weight	Number of documents	Top five terms				
Delegation	0.0564	19	delegation	tax	citizen	donors	principals
Finance and budgeting	0.0504	17	fiscal	budget	welfare	innovation	adoption
Gender and diversity	0.0504	17	women	representation	gender	womens	elected
Corruption	0.0475	16	corruption	corrupt	anticorruption	reduce	attitudes
Economic policy	0.0475	16	crisis	imf	capital	water	french
Service provision	0.0445	15	provision	collective	goods	decentralization	statehood
Supranational governance	0.0445	15	commission	executive	legislatures	member	supranational
Multilevel governance	0.0445	15	interest	groups	group	access	multilevel
Transparency	0.0415	14	transparency	foi	ngos	attitudes	limits
Organizational adaptation	0.0415	14	organizations	china	adaptation	businesses	communication

Table 7 Top ten topics in *International Public Management Journal*

Topic ID	Topic weight	Number of documents	Top five terms				
HRM	0.0800	18	job	satisfaction	leadership	commitment	fit
Networks	0.0578	13	network	networks	capacity	resource	security
Public finance	0.0533	12	financial	municipalities	municipal	incentives	production
Turnover	0.0489	11	goal	goals	turnover	actual	high
Contracting	0.0444	10	strategic	contracting	perceived	fiscal	opportunism
PSM	0.0444	10	psm	employment	bias	global	desirability
Red tape	0.0400	9	red	tape	rules	formal	rule
Health coproduction	0.0400	9	health	team	coproduction	innovation	search
Education	0.0356	8	student	principals	intrinsic	teachers	denmark
Discretion	0.0356	8	employee	discretion	integrity	choice	users

opportunism) focus on the strategic and behavioural factors that influence contracting decisions and outcomes.

The *International Review of Administrative Sciences* claims to be one of the oldest journals in public administration. It focuses on 'comparative and international topics' in public administration, especially reflections on 'international comparisons, new techniques, and approaches, academic-practice dialogue, and the future of public administration'. The topics in the journal speak to a wide array of public administration issues, such as decision-making (discretion, innovation, accountability), HRM (PSM, gender and diversity), financial management (spending) and intergovernmental or cross-sectoral relations (multi-level governance, federal government, privatisation) (see Table 8). However, this list of topics does not show whether these articles speak to the journal's aim to address comparative and international topics, partly because of the limitations of the topic modelling approach, as already noted. A content analysis of the articles is needed to determine whether the articles carry out comparative and international research.

The specific terms used to define the topics shared by the journal and the whole corpus show some nuanced differences in their focuses. For example, for the government spending topic, the whole corpus uses terms related to the broader aspects and principles of government financial management (expenditure, fund, size), whereas the terms in the journal's corpus specifically focus on the local context and specific areas of government spending (municipal, cities, police).

The *Journal of Public Administration Research and Theory* seeks to publish 'organizational, administrative, managerial, and policy-based research that improves our understanding of the public sector'. Of the ten topics identified in the analysis, red tape, street-level bureaucracy and local government are closely related to administrative research; other topics, such as networks, accountability, goal ambiguity, gender and diversity, e-government and contracting, are important topics in public organisations and management. As regulation may also be related to policy, the relationship between policy-based research and the top ten topics is generally clear (see Table 9).

Comparisons of the specific terms used in the journal and the whole corpus again reveal some nuanced differences. For example, in the whole corpus, the terms for the e-government topic (adoption, technology, media, communication) focus primarily on tools, infrastructure and the processes involved in implementing electronic government initiatives. However, the terms associated with the e-government topic in the journal's corpus (citizen satisfaction, trust, web) focus on the outcomes and citizen-centric aspects of e-government.

Table 8 Top ten topics in *International Review of Administrative Sciences*

Topic ID	Topic weight	Number of documents	Top five terms				
Innovation	0.0492	29	innovation	learning	innovations	legacy	interorganizational
Discretion	0.0441	26	welfare	politicization	discretion	clients	appointments
Gender and diversity	0.0407	24	satisfaction	career	user	analyzing	women
Spending	0.0374	22	police	municipalities	municipal	cities	spending
Privatization	0.0357	21	privatization	globalization	elites	liberalization	competitiveness
Accountability	0.0357	21	accountability	audit	expenditure	landscape	regime
PSM	0.0357	21	employees	psm	motivation	commitment	vision
Federal government	0.0340	20	commission	executive	parliament	centre	evaluations
Multilevel governance	0.0323	19	integrated	coordination	shared	canadian	fragmented
Water management	0.0306	18	integration	water	turn	mainstreaming	channels

Table 9 Top ten Topics in *Journal of Public Administration Research and Theory*

Topic ID	Topic weight	Number of documents	Top five terms				
Networks	0.0658	40	network	networks	interorganizational	scholarship	embeddedness
Regulation	0.0510	31	regulatory	business	regulation	rulemaking	content
Goal ambiguity	0.0477	29	goal	goals	ambiguity	task	clarity
Street level bureaucracy	0.0444	27	bureaucrats	clients	street level	welfare	discretion
E-government	0.0428	26	citizens	satisfaction	trust	web	e-government
Red tape	0.0395	24	job	tape	red	commitment	networking
Gender and diversity	0.0395	24	representation	active	gender	women	minority
Accountability	0.0345	21	reform	accountability	style	deregulation	measurement
Contracting	0.0345	21	contracting	contract	cost	contractors	principal
Local government	0.0329	20	municipalities	municipal	manager	crisis	climate

Local Government Studies focuses on 'local politics, policy, public adminis-tration and management and governance' and serves as an important 'forum for dialogue and exchange on local government'. Three unique topics emerged from the analysis, namely, city council, election and central–local relations, demonstrating the journal's emphasis on local politics (see Table 10). The articles in this journal also examine local governance issues related to collabor-ation (networks), finance and budgeting (public finance, spending), account-ability, transparency, leadership and e-government.

A comparison of the terms representing the shared topics in the whole corpus and the journal's corpus reveals interesting differences. For example, the leadership topic in the corpus is represented by terms like skills, style and transformational, which are related to individual characteristics, behaviours, skills and leadership styles. In contrast, in the journal corpus, the topic uses terms like officers and chief executives, which highlight the specific leadership positions that are responsible for decision-making within an organisational structure.

Public Administration is interested in articles on 'all facets of public admin-istration, public policy, and public management', especially those that deal with 'major administrative challenges that generate theoretical advances and provide substantive insights'. The top ten topics reflect the broad scope of the journal, which covers issues related to governance and regulation (networks, regula-tions, coalition, performance management and contracting), public sector man-agement (PSM, innovation and science policy) and social issues (gender and diversity and health care) (see Table 11).

A comparison of the terms used to represent the topics shared by the whole corpus and the journal's corpus shows some differences. For example, for the performance management topic, both corpora use the terms performance, measurement and indicators, indicating that these terms are integral to research on the performance management process. However, the two corpora also have some distinct focuses. The terms associated with performance management in the whole corpus include learning and improvement, highlighting the develop-mental and growth-oriented aspects of performance management. In contrast, the journal corpus includes the terms expectation and success, suggesting a focus on the alignment of performance with expectations and the attainment of successful outcomes.

Public Administration and Development states that it focuses on 'public administration at the local, regional, national and international levels where it is directed to managing development processes in low- and medium-income countries' and gives special attention to 'the management of all phases of public policy formulation and implementation' in the public and NGO sectors. Several

Table 10 Top ten topics in *Local Government Studies*

Topic ID	Topic weight	Number of documents	Top five terms				
City council	0.0520	38	councillors	participatory	group	attitudes	councillor
Networks	0.0479	35	networks	best	value	network	metagovernance
Leadership	0.0465	34	leadership	leaders	officers	chief	executives
Election	0.0438	32	party	elections	electoral	candidates	vote
Spending	0.0424	31	spending	expenditure	funding	total	resilience
E-government	0.0397	29	northern	devolution	ireland	online	egovernment
Central–local	0.0383	28	central–local	welfare	coalitions	ethnic	shift
Accountability	0.0356	26	accountability	complexity	transport	czech	balance
Public finance	0.0356	26	fiscal	revenue	tax	intergovernmental	income
Transparency	0.0356	26	information	politicians	transparency	media	spanish

Table 11 Top ten topics in *Public Administration*

Topic ID	Topic weight	Number of documents	Top five terms				
Networks	0.0551	63	network	networks	governing	modes	hierarchy
Performance management	0.0524	60	performance	measurement	expectations	success	indicators
Regulation	0.0507	58	regulatory	regulation	crisis	financial	risk
Health care	0.0490	56	health	care	nhs	knowledge	health care
Gender and diversity	0.0402	46	police	gender	rhodes	officers	representation
Coalition	0.0402	46	ireland	northern	trends	beliefs	coalition
PSM	0.0385	44	employees	motivation	psm	commitment	job
Contracting	0.0323	37	contracting	contract	contracts	procurement	relational
Innovation	0.0315	36	evaluation	innovation	adoption	municipalities	diffusion
Science policy	0.0315	36	science	germany	funding	german	blame

of the topics identified in the analysis, such as corruption, solid waste, water and environmental regulation, are important problems faced by low- and medium-income countries (see Table 12). The topics also reflect the critical role of think tanks, nonprofits, privatisation, decentralisation, finance and budgeting and benchmarking in development.

An examination of the terms representing the shared topics in the two corpora shows similarities and differences. For example, for the environmental regulation topic, the terms in the whole corpus (regulation, sustainability, water) encompass the broader concepts and principles of environmental regulation, sustainability and water management, whereas the terms in the journal's corpus (enforcement, welfare, pollution, green) highlight specific aspects of enforcement, social well-being, pollution control and environmentally friendly practices within the general topic of environmental regulation.

Public Administration Review focuses on a wide range of topics and is 'the only journal in public administration that serves both academics and practitioners interested in the public sector and public sector management'. Some of the top ten topics reflect a broad focus on institutional actors and their interactions, such as local government, nonprofits, networks and citizen participation, whereas others examine specific aspects of public sector management, such as HRM (PSM, gender and diversity, motivation, civil servant) and financial management (finance and budgeting). Interestingly, knowledge of science emerges as a unique topic for this journal, suggesting that it pays special attention to fundamental discussions of knowledge and science in the field of public administration (see Table 13).

Comparisons of the specific terms in the shared topics in the two corpora – the whole corpus versus the *PAR* articles – reveal similarities and differences in the topics. For example, for citizen participation, both corpora use such terms as citizen, participation, involvement and engagement, indicating that these terms collectively emphasise the importance of citizens' active participation in decision-making. However, the whole corpus focuses on how citizen participation is connected to democracy and legitimacy, whereas *PAR* articles highlight the interrelations between citizen participation and trust.

Public Management Review focuses on promoting 'the dissemination and discussion of such research about public management . . . across the world' and values inter-disciplinary work. The top ten topics in the *PMR* articles are HRM, innovation, performance management, networks, accountability, e-government, health care, strategic planning, sustainability and red tape (see Table 14). These topics represent different aspects of managing and improving public sector organisations, such as people management (HRM), monitoring and enhancing performance (performance management) and ensuring responsibility and

Table 12 Top ten topics in *Public Administration and Development*

Topic ID	Topic weight	Number of documents	Top five terms				
Corruption	0.0476	39	corruption	anticorruption	ethical	integrity	accs
Solid waste	0.0439	36	waste	partly	dimension	solid	msis
Nonprofits	0.0427	35	ngos	ngo	collaboration	nsps	sanitation
Decentralization	0.0415	34	decentralization	section	encouraging	ethnic	kosovo
Privatization	0.0390	32	regulatory	Privatisation	recipient	telecommunications	agricultural
Think tanks	0.0378	31	think	municipalities	chinas	tanks	caribbean
Benchmark	0.0378	31	learning	twinning	benchmarking	north	collaborative
Finance and budgeting	0.0378	31	budget	methodology	hrm	imf	budgetary
Water	0.0378	31	water	participatory	extension	agricultural	school
Environmental regulation	0.0378	31	environmental	enforcement	welfare	green	pollution

Table 13 Top ten topics in *Public Administration Review*

Topic ID	Topic weight	Number of documents	Top five terms				
Networks	0.0482	79	networks	network	collaborative	collaboration	learning
Citizen participation	0.0446	73	citizen	participation	trust	involvement	engagement
Finance and budgeting	0.0440	72	budget	fiscal	budgeting	tax	spending
Local government	0.0397	65	city	cities	county	elected	council manager
HRM	0.0366	60	satisfaction	employee	job	diversity	workplace
Civil servant	0.0360	59	civil	countries	university	china	comparative
Gender and diversity	0.0348	57	women	gender	differences	employment	men
Nonprofits	0.0336	55	nonprofit	funding	police	nonprofits	board
Motivation	0.0336	55	values	motivation	differences	commitment	mission
Knowledge of science	0.0330	54	knowledge	science	practical	scientific	fields

Table 14 Top ten topics in *Public Management Review*

Topic ID	Topic weight	Number of documents	Top five terms				
HRM	0.0612	43	employees	motivation	satisfaction	job	commitment
Innovation	0.0597	42	innovation	innovations	innovative	adoption	diffusion
Performance management	0.0512	36	performance	measures	measurement	indicators	improvement
Networks	0.0484	34	network	networks	coordination	actors	structure
Accountability	0.0455	32	accountability	regulatory	transparency	debate	charities
E-government	0.0455	32	citizens	coproduction	citizen	e-government	perceptions
Health care	0.0384	27	care	policies	involvement	professionals	patient
Strategic planning	0.0384	27	strategic	planning	strategy	branding	place
Sustainability	0.0341	24	sustainability	reporting	legitimacy	accounting	environmental
Red tape	0.0299	21	leadership	red	tape	formalization	rules

transparency (accountability). While there is considerable overlap between the top fifty topics in the whole corpus and the topics covered in this journal, two topics stand out as distinct in the journal corpus: innovation and sustainability. This indicates that the journal has a unique focus on fostering creativity and progress (innovation) in public administration and the responsible use of resources, environmental stewardship and social responsibility (sustainability).

We find subtle differences in the specific terms that characterise the shared topics in the two corpora. For example, in the whole corpus, terms for the accountability topic (expectations, responsiveness, agents) highlight the expectations placed on individuals or entities, their ability to respond to those expectations and the entities' accountability for their actions. In contrast, in the *PMR* corpus, the terms for the accountability topic (regulatory, transparency, charities) emphasise the mechanisms and practices related to ensuring accountability, including regulatory frameworks, transparency in processes and the specific accountability context of charitable organisations.

The aims and scope of *Policy & Politics* highlight research that contributes to 'existing comparative policy literature, or to policy studies, and political science more generally via the use of comparative methods'. The articles in the journal are consistent with this aim. For example, health care, urban governance, environmental regulation, inequality and welfare regimes are specific, important policy topics (see Table 15). A unique topic of the journal – policy process – reflects its focus on 'the public policy spectrum and all levels of the policy process'. Other topics in this corpus, such as networks, privatisation, partnerships and gender and diversity, are important issues in public administration and political science more generally.

There are some distinct differences between the terms representing the topics shared by the journal and the whole corpus. For example, for the urban governance topic, while both corpora focus on regeneration in an urban context, the topic in the whole corpus is represented by terms such as corruption, pay and collective, highlighting governance-related issues and practices, such as corruption prevention, fair compensation and collective decision-making, whereas the terms for the same topic in the journal's corpus (areas, diversity, communities) reflect the specific focus on neighbourhoods, the diversity of populations and the importance of community engagement in urban governance.

Public Performance and Management Review 'addresses a broad array of influential factors on the performance of public and nonprofit organizations'. The top ten topics are consistent with the stated themes of the journal, including improving budget strategies (finance and budgeting, performance budgeting), managing human resources (HRM, autonomy), building partnerships

Table 15 Top ten topics in *Policy and Politics*

Topic ID	Topic weight	Number of documents	Top five terms				
Health care	0.0681	54	health	care	mental	nhs	quality
Urban governance	0.0555	44	urban	areas	diversity	regeneration	communities
Environmental regulation	0.0492	39	european	regulation	integration	environmental	regulatory
Gender and diversity	0.0492	39	gender	women	equality	mainstreaming	practices
Inequality	0.0479	38	people	support	poverty	australian	disabled
Welfare regimes	0.0479	38	welfare	patterns	security	regimes	restructuring
Networks	0.0467	37	accountability	media	networks	agencies	network
Privatization	0.0429	34	private	business	funding	interests	initiative
Partnerships	0.0378	30	community	partnerships	working	voluntary	partnership
Policy process	0.0328	26	implementation	coordination	contemporary	action	formulation

(partnerships, networks, contracting), facilitating citizen participation (trust, local government) and applying new technologies (innovation) (see Table 16).

A comparison of the common topics shows how the specific terms differ in the two corpora. The terms representing the local government topic in the whole corpus (politicians, elected, party) focus on the individuals, processes and organisations related to governance and political representation in local government, whereas the terms in the journal's corpus (citizen, police, force) centre on community engagement, security and the roles of law enforcement agencies.

Public Money & Management covers finance, policy and management issues in public services. Among its top ten topics, accounting, finance and budgeting and cost benefits speak to the journal's focus on public finance (see Table 17), reflecting its origins in UK public finance, accounting and auditing. Other topics, such as health care, partnerships, performance management, innovation, multilevel governance and privatisation highlight the journal's attention to broader public management issues at different levels of government and across different sectors. Comparisons of the specific terms used in the whole corpus and the journal's corpus indicate that they have distinct focuses. For example, in the multilevel governance topic, both corpora have Wales and devolution, which shows that the devolution from the United Kingdom to the Welsh government is an important political issue in the area. However, the terms associated with the topic in the whole corpora include integration and governing, indicating an emphasis on the concepts and processes involved in coordinating governance across different levels of authority in multilevel governance systems, while the journal corpus has terms like Scotland and Ireland, indicating its interest in specific regional contexts within such systems and the governance arrangements and processes of those regions.

Social Policy and Administration covers social policy issues not only in Europe but also in the United States, Canada, Australia and the Asia Pacific region. The topics clearly reflect the journal's focus. For example, childcare, health care, migration, family policy, user choice, labour and employment policy and elderly care are important topics in social policy and administration (see Table 18). In addition, public finance, union and partnerships are topics that overlap with public administration. However, the international perspective is not apparent in the identified topics except the term postcommunist in the partnerships topic. Comparisons of specific terms that characterise the shared topics in the whole corpus versus the journal's corpus reveal some interesting differences in their conceptual focus. For example, the terms characterising the family policy topic in the whole corpus (administrators, identity, family) focus on the institutions, concepts and dynamics related to policymaking and implementation in the context of families, whereas those in the journal's corpus

Table 16 Top ten topics in *Public Performance and Management Review*

Topic ID	Topic weight	Number of documents	Top five terms				
Partnerships	0.0842	23	business	ppp	ppps	partnerships	bids
Performance budgeting	0.0549	15	measurement	budgeting	pbb	requirements	laws
Networks	0.0476	13	network	networks	health	interorganizational	response
Trust	0.0440	12	trust	care	interorganizational	partners	distrust
Local government	0.0403	11	citizen	city	municipalities	force	police
HRM	0.0403	11	satisfaction	job	emotional	labor	media
Autonomy	0.0366	10	autonomy	control	target	corruption	setting
Contracting	0.0366	10	contract	contracting	contracts	intergovernmental	competitive
Finance and budgeting	0.0366	10	fiscal	stress	outsourcing	austerity	environment
Innovation	0.0330	9	perceptions	culture	bureaucracy	innovative	innovation

Table 17 Top ten topics in *Public Money and Management*

Topic ID	Topic weight	Number of documents	Top five terms				
Accounting	0.0681	74	accounting	reporting	accountability	standards	resource
Health care	0.0617	67	health	care	nhs	trust	trusts
Local government	0.0571	62	local	authorities	england	authority	council
Partnerships	0.0451	49	procurement	ppps	partnerships	ppp	partnership
Performance management	0.0451	49	performance	indicators	systems	measurement	evaluation
Multilevel governance	0.0396	43	wales	devolution	ireland	scottish	scotland
Finance and budgeting	0.0387	42	private	finance	pfi	projects	money
Cost-benefits	0.0378	41	costs	cost	efficiency	funding	benefits
Innovation	0.0368	40	implementation	innovation	lean	improvement	challenges
Privatization	0.0341	37	transport	privatization	problems	rail	industry

Table 18 Top ten topics in *Social Policy and Administration*

Topic ID	Topic weight	Number of documents	Top five terms				
Health care	0.0618	64	nhs	medical	criteria	practitioners	ireland
Public finance	0.0425	44	pension	rural	plans	fund	oldage
Childcare	0.0415	43	child	childcare	childrens	promotion	diffusion
Migration	0.0396	41	china	urban	migration	chinese	hong
Family policy	0.0396	41	parents	lone	cent	workfare	mothers
User choice	0.0386	40	users	user	projects	female	joint
Union	0.0367	38	health care	occupational	unions	class	dualization
Partnerships	0.0367	38	partnership	partnerships	privatization	parental	postcommunist
Labor and employment policy	0.0338	35	activation	attitudes	unemployed	programme	claimants
Elderly care	0.0338	35	older	carers	homes	households	nursing

(parents, lone, workfare, mothers) pay more attention to various aspects of family structures, roles and support systems within family policy.

3.3 Comparing Journal Topics

We also examined which topics were common across the peer-reviewed journals in our corpus, or the stock of topics within all journals, and the variation in the journals' specific focuses within these topics, or the stock of topics by journal. Table 19 lists the thirty-eight topics that occur in the topic list for the whole corpus and for at least one journal. Some topics were extensively studied in multiple academic journals, indicating that they are fundamental issues that public administration scholars consistently examine. For example, networks appeared in nine journals' top ten topics. Gender and diversity and health care were among the top ten topics in seven journals. These recurring themes reflect a common consensus within the field. However, some topics, although ranked among the top topics in the whole corpus, were niche topics specific to particular academic journals. For example, family policy and labour and employment policy only appeared in the top ten topics list of *SPA*. Inequality and welfare regimes were only among the top ten topics for *P&P*. These specialised areas of research cater to the specific interests, aims, scopes and focuses of those journals and illustrate the variety of topics and academic publication outlets in the discipline.

To further examine how the widely studied topics were approached by different academic journals, we zoomed in on the topics that appeared in the top ten topic lists of at least five journals, that is, networks (in nine journals), gender and diversity (in seven journals), health care (in seven journals), partnerships (in six journals), HRM (in five journals), finance and budgeting (in five journals) and privatisation (in five journals). We examined the extent to which common terms are used among public administration journals by calculating the percentage of journals that shared the same terms in their topics. Specific terms in the topics are also listed by journals in Table 19.

Networks was the most widely studied topic. It appeared as one of the top ten topics in over 50% of the sample journals (in nine journals). The terms 'network' and 'networks' were among the top five terms characterising the topic in all of these journals (100%). Despite the common interest, these journals had specific focuses within the network topic. Some journals examined actors and governance structures in the networks, featuring terms like actors (*PMR*), agencies (*P&P*), structure (*PMR*), modes (*PA*), hierarchy (*PA*) and metagovernance (*LGS*). Some journals, especially *IPMJ*, paid more attention to resources in network management, as evidenced in the prominence of terms

Table 19 Topic comparison across public administration academic journals

#	Topics	# of journals	Common terms	Journal and specific terms in the topic
1	Networks	9	Network (100%), networks (100%)	*ARPA* (coordination, disaster, ties), *IPMJ* (capacity, resource, security), *JPART* (interorganization, scholarship, embeddedness), *LGS* (best, value, metagovernance), *PA* (governing, modes, hierarchy), *PAR* (collaborative, collaboration, learning), *PMR* (coordination, actors, structure), *P&P* (accountability, media, agencies), *PPMR* (health, interorganizational, response)
2	Gender and diversity	7	Gender (86%), women (86%) Representation (57%)	*A&S* (officials, representation, professional), Governance (representation, elected), *IRAS* (satisfaction, career, user, analyzing), *JPART* (representation, active, minority), *PA* (police, officers, representation), *PAR* (differences, employment, men), *P&P* (equality, practices, mainstreaming)
3	Health care	7	Health (71%) Care (86%) NHS (57%)	*A&S* (managers, strategic, strategies), *EPC* (decentralization, devolution, welfare), *PA* (nhs, knowledge),

Table 19 (cont.)

#	Topics	# of journals	Common terms	Journal and specific terms in the topic
4	Partnerships	6	Partnership (83%) Partnerships (100%)	*PMR* (policies, involvement, professionals, patient), *P&P* (mental, nhs, quality), Public Money & Management (nhs, trust, trusts), *SPA* (nhs, medical, practitioners, criteria, Ireland) *ARPA* (collaborative, collaboration, stakeholder) *EPC* (regeneration, member), *P&P* (community, working, voluntary), *PPMR* (business, PPP, bids), *PMM* (procurement, PPP), *SPA* (privatization, parental, postcommunist)
5	HRM	5	Job (100%) Satisfaction (80%) Employee (60%)	*A&S* (performance, relationships, employees, attitudes), *IPMJ* (satisfaction, leadership, commitment, fit), *PAR* (satisfaction, employee, diversity, workplace), *PMR* (employees, motivation, satisfaction, commitment), *PPMR* (satisfaction, emotional, labor, media)
6	Finance and budgeting	5	Fiscal (80%) Budget (60%)	*EPC* (fiscal, decentralization, expenditure, revenue, intergovernmental), Governance (fiscal, budget, welfare, innovation,adoption), *PAD* (budget, methodology, hrm, imf, budgetary),

#	Topic		Count	Keywords
7	Privatization	Privatization (60%)	5	*PAR (budget, fiscal, budgeting, tax, spending), PPMR (fiscal, stress, outsourcing, austerity, environment) EPC (enterprise, ethnic, training, assistance, advice), IRAS (privatization, globalization, elites, liberalization, competitiveness), PAD (regulatory, privatisation, recipient, telecommunications, agricultural), P&P (private, business, funding, interests, initiative), PMM (transport, privatization, problems, rail, industry)*
8	Nonprofits		4	*A&S, ARPA, PAD, PAR*
9	PSM		4	*ARPA, IPMJ, IRAS, PA*
10	e-government		4	*JPART, LGS, PMR, ARPA*
11	Local government		4	*ARPA, PAR, PPMR, PMM*
12	Public finance		4	*EPC, IPMJ, LGS, SPA*
13	Contracting		4	*IPMJ, JPART, PA, PPMR*
14	Multilevel governance		3	*Governance, IRAS, PMM*
15	Red tape		3	*IPMJ, JPART, PMR*
16	Performance management		3	*PA, PMR, PMM*
17	Citizen participation		2	*A&S, PAR*
18	Education		2	*A&S, IPMJ*
19	Welfare		2	*A&S, P&P*
20	Strategic planning		2	*ARPA, PMR*
21	Spending		2	*IRAS, LGS*

Table 19 (cont.)

#	Topics	# of journals	Common terms	Journal and specific terms in the topic
22	Accountability	2		*IRAS, PMR*
23	Environmental regulation	2		*PAD, P&P*
24	Civil servant	2		*A&S, PAR*
25	Transparency	2		*LGS, Governance*
26	Representative bureaucracy	1		*ARPA*
27	Regional governance	1		*EPC*
28	Federal government	1		*IRAS*
29	Leadership	1		*LGS*
30	Science policy	1		*PA*
31	Decentralization	1		*PAD*
32	Urban governance	1		*P&P*
33	Inequality	1		*P&P*
34	Welfare regime	1		*P&P*
35	Autonomy	1		*PPMR*
36	Family policy	1		*SPA*
37	Labor and employment policy	1		*SPA*
38	User choice	1		*SPA*

Note: The percentages in the parentheses indicate the percentage of journals that shared the same terms in their topics.

like capacity and resources. Other journals focused on network processes and dynamics – the interactions, collaborations and relationships within networks, represented by terms like coordination (*ARPA*, *PMR*), collaboration (*PAR*), interorganisational (*JPART*, *PPMR*), learning (*PAR*) and accountability (*P&P*). In addition, research on network was conducted in diverse contexts. Terms like disaster (*ARPA*), health (*PPMR*) and media (*P&P*) highlighted the specific domains or sectors where networks operate and the specific challenges and dynamics within those contexts.

Gender and diversity was the second most widely studied topic in our corpus of public administration journals, with seven journals featuring this topic as one of their top ten topics. Researchers examined the dynamics of gender equality and the representation of women and minority groups, as indicated by the terms gender (86%), women (86%) and representation (57%). A closer look at the specific terms in the journals' topic definitions revealed the different lines of research and the nuanced difference in the journals' focuses. For example, some studies examined how public administrators, especially elected officials (*A&S*, *Governance*), police officers (*PA*) and professionals (*A&S*) treat minorities (*JPART*), men (*PAR*) and public service users (*IRAS*) in different ways in various settings, such as employment (*PAR*), career development (*IRAS*) and public service delivery practices (*P&P*). These studies focused on how these differential treatments are related to differences (*PAR*), equality (*P&P*) and satisfaction (*IRAS*). While some journals, such as *IRAS* and *PAR*, focused on representation in hiring and promotion in the workplace, most journals, such as *A&S*, *Governance*, *JPART*, *PA* and *P&P*, examined how different minority groups are treated in service delivery.

Similar to the gender and diversity topic, seven public administration journals had health care as one of their top ten topics. These journals commonly used the terms health (71%) and care (86%), with particular attention paid to the United Kingdom's National Health Service (NHS) (57%). Despite the common focus, these journals focused on different issues in health care. For example, journals like *P&P* and *SPA* focused on how to ensure the quality of care and used specific criteria to evaluate the effectiveness of care provided by medical practitioners, particularly in the realm of mental health. Some journals, such as *PMM* and *EPC*, paid more attention to health care reforms, as evidenced by the frequency of terms like devolution and decentralisation. The decentralisation reform in the NHS, part of which revolved around the establishment of trusts, has had a significant impact on the delivery of welfare and health care services. Other journals, such as *PMR* and *A&S*, focused on how managers design and implement strategies and policies, such as the involvement of health care professionals and patients, to enhance patient care and outcomes.

Partnerships featured as a topic in six journals, and the terms partnership (83%) and its plural form (100%) appeared frequently in the top five terms characterising the topic. By looking into the specific terms that represent the topic in different corpora, we found that a recurring theme in the journals was stakeholder collaborations, such as those among communities, businesses, members and parents, in diverse settings, such as regeneration. Another line of research examined procurement, bids and privatisation – the technical and financial aspects of partnerships. Compared with studies on other topics (e.g., networks), which were often quite diffuse, our analysis suggests that studies on partnerships were relatively focused.

Five journals covered HRM topics extensively, and the terms shared by the topic in these journals included job (100%), satisfaction (80%) and employee (60%), reflecting the topic's overall focus on employee and job satisfaction. Zooming in on the specific terms representing the topic, we found that these journals consistently focused on employee attitudes, commitment, satisfaction and emotional labour in the workplace. There were also some studies of leadership, diversity and person–organisation fit, and how these factors shape job attitude and performance.

Finance and budgeting figured extensively in five public administration journals. Fiscal (80%) and budget (60%) were two common terms representing the topic. A detailed examination of the specific terms across journals showed that studies on finance and budgeting were clearly focused on either the broader management of public finances, such as revenue generation (tax, outsourcing, stress), expenditure control (expenditure, spending) and overall financial policy (decentralisation, intergovernmental, innovation, adoption), or the allocation of financial resources, such as creating, implementing and monitoring funds.

Privatisation was a topic included in the top ten topics of five public administration journals, with the term privatisation appearing in three journals' topic terms. However, the specific terms used in different journals indicated the different lines of research. One line of research examined the broader economic impact of privatisation, including globalisation, liberalisation and efforts to enhance competitiveness. Another line of inquiry focused on regulatory frameworks and the stakeholders involved in the privatisation process, such as businesses, elites and recipients. The studies of privatisation were conducted in diverse sectors, such as telecommunication, transportation, agriculture, infrastructure and energy.

All seventeen journals published articles on the seven most popular topics in the inter-journal analysis. *Policy and Politics* included articles on these inter-journal topics most frequently, on five occasions (networks, gender and diversity, health care, partnerships, privatisation). Two journals published four of the topics: *PAR* (networks, gender and diversity, HRM, finance and budgeting) and *PPMR* (networks, partnerships, HRM, finance and budgeting). Four journals published on two of these topics: *Governance* (gender and diversity, finance and budgeting), *IRAS* (gender and diversity, privatisation), *PAD* (finance and budgeting, privatisation) and *SPA* (health care, partnerships). This suggests a wider diversity of published topics in these journals, seen by single topics in these journals such as federal government (*IRAS*), decentralisation (*PAD*) and family policy, labour and employment policy and user choice (*SPA*).

4 Changes in Topics in Public Administration

To examine the chronology of topics over time we examined the flows or movement in topics by first examining the variation in topic weights between 1991 and 2019 and also conducted keyness analysis to contrast topics in the early period in our corpus – the first five years – with the late period – the last five years.

4.1 Changing Topic Weights

As the number of published articles varied significantly across years, we calculated the topic prominence by using all of the articles on a certain topic published in a year divided by the total number of articles published annually in the seventeen journals for the 1991–2019 period. This presents the flow of topics over time. Figure 2 presents the changes in the relative prominence of the top ten topics over the study period. On average, these topics were examined in approximately 3% of the articles every year, with peaks and lows for different topics.

Health care emerged as a highly topical subject during the late 1980s, with approximately 15% of all articles dedicated to health-related topics. This surge can be attributed to the widespread health care reforms implemented in the United Kingdom and other nations. However, in the subsequent decade, the prominence of health care experienced a noticeable decline, with minor fluctuations between 1995 and the early 2000s. Health care issues regained prominence in 2008, likely due to the implementation of the Obama Care reform in the United States. The prevalence of this issue gradually diminished after 2010.

Research on the federal government gained momentum in the 1990s and reached its zenith in 1995. Subsequently, there were fluctuations in the number of studies, culminating in another significant peak in 2008. This resurgence can be attributed to the profound impact of the Great Recession, which ignited fervent debates on the role of federal government in both economic development and governance.

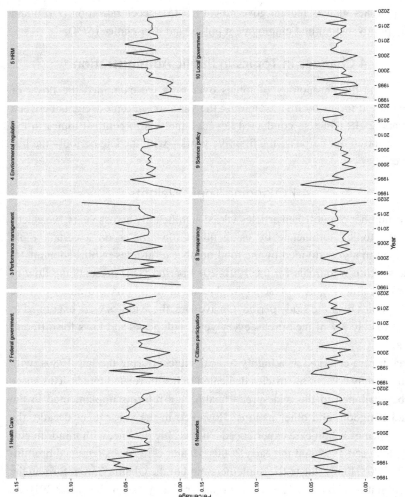

Figure 2 Evolution of the top one to ten topics in public administration

Research on performance management increased significantly in the 1990s and peaked in 1995. After small fluctuations between 1995 and 2013, the relative number of studies on performance management have been growing at a rapid rate since 2014. This sharp growth can be largely attributed to the series of government reforms in performance management in different countries following the NPM movement. For example, in 2013, the US government promulgated the GPRA Modernization Act, which retains and amplifies some features of the Government Performance and Results Act of 1993 (GPRA 1993) while also addressing some of its weaknesses. The more recent growth in this topic could be accounted for by the advent of behavioural public administration, much of which focuses on the use of performance information in public organisations and by citizens.

The prominence of research on environmental regulations has been relatively stable, except for the sharp growth between 1990 and 1995, probably because of the dedicated policy attention to environmental issues, as evidenced by the Rio Earth Summit in 1992 and other international events, which triggered increased global awareness and action to address environmental issues and the development and implementation of various regulations and agreements. In addition, interest in environmental regulations peaked a second time around 2016, probably because of the Paris Agreement and other global environmental treaties.

Research on HRM has slowly gained prominence since the 1990s and gained momentum in 2002, probably because the Federal Employee Viewpoint Survey was first conducted in 2002 to assess the views and experiences of federal employees. This suggests that data availability is critical to scholarship.

Research on networks was very popular in the 1980s and declined sharply in the 1990s, after which the relative volume of studies on the topic has been stable. Interestingly, the pattern for health care and networks was similar: both experienced a noticeable decline after a period of prominence in the 1980s. The prominence of articles on citizen participation and transparency exhibited similar patterns: substantial growth in the 1990s, followed by minor fluctuations in later years.

Studies of science policy increased around 1993, and then quickly declined. The peak can likely be attributed to the development of the Information Superhighway in the United States, as evidenced by the significant expansion of Internet access, advancements in digital technologies and the rise of the World Wide Web. During this period, there was a surge of public interest in and policy discussions surrounding the development and use of the Information Superhighway. Interest in local government gained momentum in 2002, following a similar pattern to that of HRM.

Figure 3 shows the flow of the evolution of the topics ranked as the eleventh to twentieth most popular in the whole corpus. Interest in research on welfare

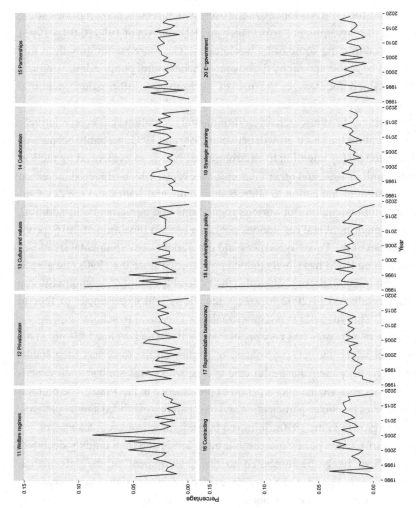

Figure 3 Evolution of the top eleven to twenty topics in public administration

regimes fluctuated every two to three years and then gained momentum in 2005, probably because of the welfare regimes introduced in many countries in 2002 and 2003, such as the social assistance programme and urban social insurance reforms in China. Studies on culture and values were very prominent at the beginning of our study period but interest sharply declined in the early 1990s, followed by downward fluctuations, suggesting that interest in this area of research is shrinking.

Research on privatisation, collaboration, partnerships and contracting has remained relatively stable, with small fluctuations, probably because these topics are fragmented. Interest in representative bureaucracy has shown a slow, steady increase, suggesting that this topic is becoming more popular in the field as questions about diversity, gender and race figure prominently in the public discourses of many societies and are being reflected in scholarship.

Research on labour and employment policy experienced a dramatic decline in the early 1990s, followed by a relatively stable development. Two reasons may have contributed to this trend. First, certain social, policy and welfare changes may have promoted interest in labour and employment policy in public administration in the late 1980s to early 1990s. Second, scholarship on labour and employment policies may have moved from public administration to other fields, such as economics, leading to the decline in the number of studies published in public administration journals.

The number of studies on strategic planning has remained relatively stable, with small fluctuations. Interestingly, small peaks occurred approximately every five years, suggesting that it often takes time for strategic problems and issues to emerge and for strategies to be developed and implemented. Interest in e-government has also been relatively stable, but with a noticeable peak in 1997. Certain significant events and milestones related to e-government, such as the use of World Wide Web and the Government Paperwork Elimination Act in the United States (1998), may have laid the foundation for the digital transformation of government services and the adoption of e-government practices.

Figure 4 shows the evolution of interest in the twenty-first to thirtieth most popular topics in the whole corpus. Research on gender and diversity experienced a moderate decline in the early 1990s and remained low for about five years, bouncing back in 1997. The number of studies on the topic has remained relatively stable since the 2000s, with minor fluctuations. The topics of public finance, finance/budgeting and development aid exhibited largely similar patterns: small peaks in the 2000–2005 period, followed by stability. Research on nonprofits had a large peak in 1993, followed by small peaks in 2000 and 2015.

Interest in the topic of senior civil servants was low throughout the study period, except for peaks in 1990 and 2010. The two peaks may have been driven

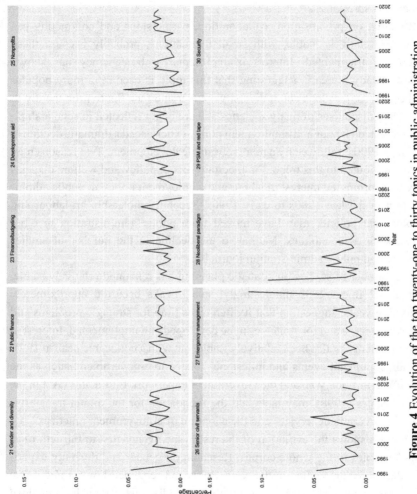

Figure 4 Evolution of the top twenty-one to thirty topics in public administration

by reform efforts made in those years to enhance the professionalism, effectiveness and accountability of senior civil servants.

Emergency management had generally low prominence but has experienced sharp growth since 2013. The combination of increased disaster events, the impact of climate change, technological advancements, policy changes and a growing recognition of the interdisciplinary nature of emergency management may have contributed to the rise in the relative number of studies on emergency management after 2013.

Research using a neoliberal paradigm was very popular in the late 1980s and early 1990s. As an important theoretical foundation for NPM, the neoliberal paradigm was heatedly discussed at that time. However, as interest in NPM waned, studies of the neoliberal paradigm declined significantly and have remained low since the 2000s, with small peaks occurring every five years. However, work has continued in a number of topics related to aspects of NPM, such as performance management. Research on PSM and red tape was relatively stable from the 1990s to 2017 but has increased significantly since then. The growing number of studies on PSM since 2017 indicates the reviving interest in the field. The relative volume of studies on security remained stable across the study period.

Figure 5 shows the evolution of the thirty-first to fortieth most popular topics. The relative prominence of research in education, urban governance, local decentralisation and leadership exhibited similar patterns: stable with minor fluctuations. The relative prominence of studies on regional governance and urban governance peaked at nearly the same time – around 2000. Research on accountability and inequality showed similar patterns, with some peaks in the early 2000s, and substantial growth after 2015. The surge in research on accountability and inequality may be driven by global governance reforms, international development agendas such as the UN Sustainable Development Goals and high-profile scandals.

Research on spending peaked in the 1990s, followed by a sharp decline in the late 1990s and then a stable pattern. Interest at the peak was probably associated with the prevalence of NPM, a management philosophy and set of principles that aim to improve the efficiency, effectiveness and accountability of public sector organisations, including their use of financial resources. Research on economic policy has been decreasing overall in the public administration field, probably because the topic has become more salient in other fields, such as economics. Research on Europe was relatively stable throughout the study period, with a peak around 2007, probably because of the several key events, such as the Treaty of Lisbon, EU enlargement, the 2008 financial crisis and ongoing debates on European identity.

In Figure 6, we show the evolution of research in the ten least popular topics. Research on multilevel governance, family policy, risk management and

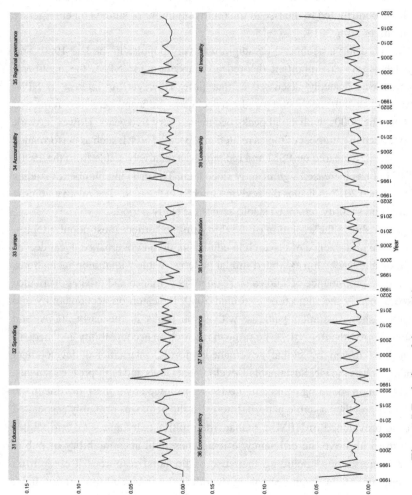

Figure 5 Evolution of the top thirty-one to forty topics in public administration

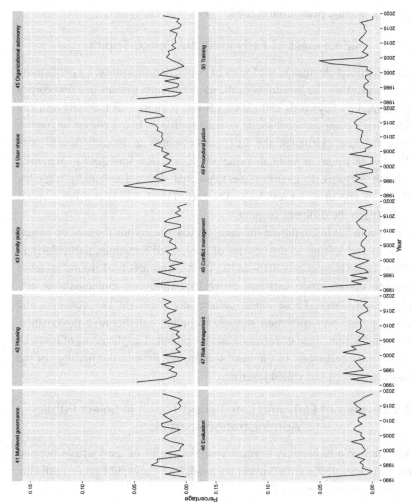

Figure 6 Evolution of the top forty-one to fifty topics in public administration

procedural justice has been relatively stable with minor fluctuations. The prominence of research in housing, organisational autonomy, evaluation and conflict management exhibited similar patterns: a sharp decline in the early 1990s, followed by small fluctuations. The large volume of studies on organisational autonomy and evaluation in the early 1990s was probably related to the NPM reforms. Studies on training remained rare throughout the study period except for a notable peak around 2004.

4.2 Keyness of Early and Late Period Topics

We also examined changes in the topics of public administration by performing a keyness analysis – the aboutness or the most common themes in a text corpus as represented by keywords and their LLR and p-value – of the early and late periods using a computational social science approach. In our corpus linguistics analysis, we first calculated the LLR of keywords to identify words with a *p*-level <.001 and a critical value of 15.13 (Rayson 2008). We used WordSmith software to examine the keywords with an unusually high log likelihood of appearing in articles in the early (1991–1995) and late periods (2015–2019) in the different corpora.

As shown in Table 20, during the early period, the corpus focused on issues, experiences and lessons in the context of the United Kingdom, particularly in the 1980s. In the late period (2015–2019), discussions revolved around issues of governance, collaboration, citizens, networks, employees, municipalities, actors and practitioners. These topics collectively highlight key concepts and themes in public administration studies, including collaborative governance, citizen participation, local governance and the practical implications of research for real-world challenges. In the next section, we present the findings of the keyness analyses of individual journals.

4.3 Keyness of Early and Late Period Topics in Select Public Administration Journals

We were not able to conduct keyness analyses for all of the journals because eleven of the seventeen journals in our corpus did not begin publication until after 1991. We therefore examined *EPC*, *PA*, *PAD*, *PAR*, *P&P* and *SPA*. Table 21 presents the results of the journal-level keyness analysis of all articles published by *EPC*. In the early period, the corpus did not have a clear focus, whereas in the late period, key themes emerged, including governance, climate, water, environmental, networks and actors. These keywords reflect the journal's focus on politics and space, highlighting the interdisciplinary nature of environmental governance, which involves multiple stakeholders, policy domains and complex

Table 20 Keyness comparison between (1991–1995) and (2015–2019) in corpus

1991–1995				2015–2019			
Keyword	Freq.	Reference corpus freq.	Log-likelihood	Keyword	Freq.	Reference corpus freq.	Log-likelihood
1980s	64	31	89.92	Governance	900	40	234.85
Britain	58	25	87.13	Collaborative	322	8	107.88
British	70	44	82.51	Citizens	469	30	95.78
				Networks	369	19	88.15
				Employees	408	26	83.58
				Municipalities	282	14	68.94
				Actors	353	27	61.44
				Practitioners	276	21	48.29

Note: The ranking is based on log likelihood scores and all the scores are significant at $p < 0.001$.

Table 21 Keyness comparison between (1991–1995) and (2015–2019) in *Environment and Planning C*

Environment and Planning C articles (1991–1995)				Environment and Planning C articles (2015–2019)			
		Reference corpus				Reference corpus	
Keyword	Freq.	freq. (2015–2019)	Log-likelihood	Keyword	Freq.	freq. (1991–1995)	Log-likelihood
EC	18	0	33.63	Governance	134	4	105.01
				Climate	68	1	59.29
				Water	34	0	33.94
				Environmental	83	12	33.2
				Networks	40	1	32.39
				Actors	47	3	29.82

environmental challenges, as well as the importance of collaboration, policy coordination and the active participation of key actors to address environmental and climate issues.

Our keyness analysis of *PA* showed that in the early period, the journal discussed issues relating to expenditure, Britain and the NHS, reflecting the massive health care reform implemented in the United Kingdom and issues related to government expenditures (Table 22). In the late period, the journal focused on coordination, performance and citizens, demonstrating the importance of coordination among diverse actors, performance assessment for effective governance and the role of citizens as key stakeholders in shaping public policies and administration. The keyness analysis captured the journal's focus in the late period on 'facets of public administration, public policy, and public management'.

The keyness analysis of the articles published by *PAD* in the early period showed that the corpus was characterised by terms like planning, environmental, projects, agricultural, training and privatisation (Table 23). These terms collectively highlight various dimensions in the field of development, including the importance of planning for sustainable development, the integration of environmental concerns, the implementation of development projects, the significance of agricultural development, the role of training in capacity building and the potential impacts of privatisation on development outcomes. In the late period, the journal became more focused, and the key terms included terms like police, policing and governance, illustrating the journal's considerable attention to policing and governance issues. These topics somewhat contrast with the aims of the journal, which are to examine 'the management of all phases of public policy formulation and implementation'.

Table 24 presents the results of the keyness analysis of the articles published in *PAR*. In the early period, administrators stood out as a keyword in the corpus. However, in the late period, the journal focused on issues related to performance, citizens, police, actors, evidence and collaboration, which collectively show the journal's focus on a broad range of issues in public administration, such as performance measurement and management, the role of citizens, the management of law enforcement agencies, the use of evidence in decision-making and collaborative approaches to governance and service delivery. The keyness analysis reflected the journal's current broad aims and scope.

Our keyness analysis of *P&P* revealed a strong focus on policy issues, in particular those related to health and housing, between 1991 and 1995 (Table 25), which shifted in the late period to issues of media, governance and public, highlighting the journal's attention to the role of the media in shaping policy discourse and public opinion, the significance of governance in policy

Table 22 Keyness comparison between (1991–1995) and (2015–2019) in *Public Administration*

| | *PA* articles (1991–1995) | | | | *PA* articles (2015–2019) | | |
| | | Reference corpus | | | | Reference corpus | |
Keyword	Freq.	freq. (2015–2019)	Log-likelihood	Keyword	Freq.	freq. (1991–1995)	Log-likelihood
Expenditure	20	0	47.79	Coordination	53	1	30.66
British	24	4	37.26	Performance	120	14	30.29
NHS	21	3	34.25	Citizens	41	0	29.58

Note: The ranking is based on log likelihood scores and all the scores are significant at $p < 0.001$.

Table 23 Keyness comparison between (1991–1995) and (2015–2019) in *Public Administration and Development*

| | *PAD* articles (1991–1995) | | | | *PAD* articles (2015–2019) | | |
| | Reference corpus | | | | Reference corpus | | |
Keyword	Freq.	freq. (2015–2019)	Log-likelihood	Keyword	Freq.	freq. (1991–1995)	Log-likelihood
Planning	38	0	43.01	Police	39	0	65.43
Environmental	41	2	33.59	Policing	19	0	31.88
Projects	40	2	32.55	Governance	42	11	28.79
Agricultural	27	0	39.12				
Training	38	2	30.49				
Privatization	26	0	29.43				

Note: The ranking is based on log likelihood scores and all the scores are significant at $p < 0.001$.

Table 24 Keyness comparison between (1991–1995) and (2015–2019) in *Public Administration Review*

| *PAR* articles (1991–1995) | | | *PAR* articles (2015–2019) | | | |
Keyword	Freq.	Reference corpus freq. (2015–2019)	Log-likelihood	Keyword	Freq.	Reference corpus freq. (1991–1995)	Log-likelihood
Administrators	33	22	30.02	Performance	204	39	59.63
				Citizens	58	1	48.52
				Police	47	1	38.18
				Actors	35	0	34.25
				Evidence	101	17	33.83
				Collaborative	32	0	31.32

Table 25 Keyness comparison between (1991–1995) and (2015–2019) in *Policy & Politics*

| | *Policy & Politics* articles (1991–1995) | | | | *Policy & Politics* articles (2015–2019) | | |
| | | Reference corpus | | | | Reference corpus | |
Keyword	Freq.	freq. (2015–2019)	Log-likelihood	Keyword	Freq.	freq. (1991–1995)	Log-likelihood
Health	67	9	66.36	Media	45	0	51.48
Housing	35	5	33.75	Governance	58	4	43.34
				Public	104	27	30.56

processes and the centrality of the public as both recipients and active partici-
pants in public services and policies. These keyness terms in the late period
clearly captured the journal's focus on policy studies but did not tease out its
comparative research and methods aims.

The final journal that published throughout our study period was *SPA* and our
analysis showed a reduction in the number of keyness terms from three to one –
the only other journal to show this pattern was *PAD* (Table 26). During the early
period, the corpus was characterised by the terms medical, police and NHS.
These terms collectively demonstrate the importance of social policy in
addressing health care and public service-related concerns. In the late period,
one keyword emerged from the corpus – countries – suggesting that the journal
paid considerable attention to cross-country comparison in studies in that
period, reflecting the journal's aims to examine the social policies of different
countries.

5 Geography of Topics in Public Administration

To examine the distribution of topics over space, we conducted our analysis of
the World Bank Governance Indicators in three steps. First, we identified which
World Bank Governance Indicator each of the fifty topics of public administration aligned with. As well as identifying the stock of topics associated with each
indicator, we also examined the flow of these topics over time by examining the
changing topic weight for each of the World Bank Governance Indicators.
Second, we compared the relative prominence of the six governance indicators
in countries with low versus high scores on the World Bank Governance
Indicators. Third, we listed a maximum of the top five topics associated with
each indicator category and compared the similarities and differences in the
prominence of topics examined in countries with low (versus high) governance
scores.

Nearly half (twenty-four) of the public administration topics were associated
with the indicator government effectiveness (Table 27), accounting for 49.6% of
the research by TW. This is perhaps to be expected, given public administration's focus on the administration and management of government and policy
consequences. The twenty-four topics capture these processes and examine
people management, structures and management processes, budgeting, networks and partnerships and the broader context of governance. The second
most popular World Bank Governance Indicator was voice and accountability,
which was aligned with seven topics (14% of the topics accounting for 13.7% of
TW), and included an emphasis on citizens, representation, diversity and
accountability. Ten topics were distributed across the remaining four World

Table 26 Keyness comparison between (1991–1995) and (2015–2019) in *Social Policy and Administration*

Social Policy and Administration articles (1991–1995)			*Social Policy and Administration* articles (2015–2019)			
Keyword	Freq.	Reference corpus freq. (2015–2019)	Log-likelihood	Keyword	Freq.	Reference corpus freq. (1991–1995)	Log-likelihood
Medical	15	2	43.99	Countries	173	6	28.63
Police	12	1	37.79				
NHS	15	7	30.49				

Table 27 Topic categories based on World Bank Governance Indicator

Higher level category	Topic weights	Topics: Fifty topics of public administration
Control of corruption	1.5	urban governance
Government effectiveness	49.6	federal government, performance management, HRM, networks, local government, culture and values, collaboration, partnerships, strategic planning, e-government, public finance, finance/budgeting, senior civil servants, emergency management, neoliberal paradigm, PSM and red tape, spending, regional governance, local decentralization, leadership, multilevel governance, evaluation, training
Political stability	3.8	security, risk management, conflict management
Regulatory quality	10.2	environmental regulation, welfare regimes, privatization, contracting
Rule of law	4.6	labor/employment policy, economic policy, procedural justice
Voice and accountability	13.7	citizen participation, transparency, representative bureaucracy, gender and diversity, accountability, user choice, organizational autonomy
Unknown	17.6	health care, science policy, development aid, nonprofits, education, europe, inequality, housing, family policy

Bank Governance Indicator categories. The control of corruption indicator was associated with one topic – urban governance (TW = 1.5%) – while the political stability (TW = 3.8%) and the rule of law (TW = 4.6%) indicators were associated with seven topics. The regulatory quality indicator captured four topics (TW = 10.2%), suggesting the importance of regulatory processes in environmental welfare and privatisation. Finally, nine topics (18%; TW = 17.6%) did not neatly match any of the World Bank Governance Indicator categories and were classified as 'unknown'. This included the most common topic in public administration – health care – in addition to policy areas such as family, housing and science policy.

Figure 7 presents the topic weights over time for each of the World Bank Governance Indicator categories, plus those classified as unknown. This visualisation clearly draws out how the balance of scholarship is distributed across the six indicators. The flow of scholars writing on topics that align with the control of corruption and political stability shows relatively little fluctuation, with occasional increases in the percent of topic weights. Scholarship on regulatory quality reach a peak around 2005 and has been in steady decline since. This may reflect the establishment of journals such as *Regulation & Governance* which was established in 2007, and where scholars working on these themes may now direct their work.

Topics associated with the rule of law were popular at the beginning of our time period, but the flow of work authored on topics relating to this World Bank Governance Indicator category has persistently remained around 0.05% of topics since then. Topic weights were high for the category of voice and accountability, with a peak of publication in the late 1990s and remained relatively constant since then with a small uptake in publication in recent years. The World Bank Governance Indicator category of government effectiveness, the category most associated with topics in our corpus of all journals, has shown the largest fluctuation in the flows of publication ranging nearly 0.2% of topic weights. Research on government effectiveness reached two peaks of publication between 2000–2010 and was rising again at the end of our study period in 2019.

5.1 World Bank Governance Indicator Categories and Topics

The proportion of the corpus focused on each of the six World Bank Governance Indicator categories broadly reflected the overall pattern of topics in the corpus, as shown in Table 27. The rank order of the six indicators (Table 28) was government effectiveness, voice and accountability, regulatory quality, rule of law, political stability and control of corruption. However, there were variations in topic weights for countries with low and high governance scores. In our analysis, we highlighted differences in topic weights equal to or greater than 1% between low-and high-scoring countries and within each of the indicators. Here, we discuss differences in the top five topic terms. (A detailed analysis of the topics within each indicator is presented in Appendix tables A1–A6.)

In countries/territories scoring low in control of corruption, government effectiveness accounted for nearly 50% of research by topic weight (49.9%), which was 1.8% higher than in high-scoring countries. Among the top five topics in each

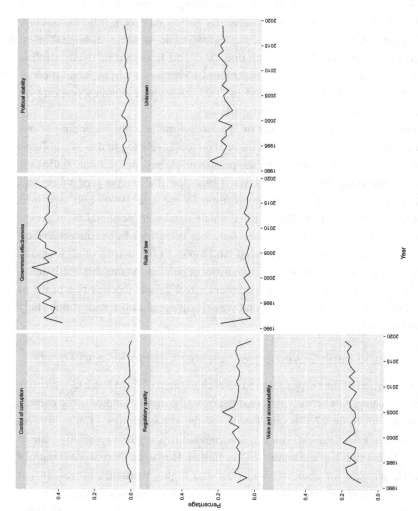

Figure 7 Changes in topic weights in WBGI categories

Table 28 Topics comparison between countries scoring low and high in across the World Bank Governance Indicators

	Countries scoring low			Countries scoring high	
	#	%		#	%
	Government corruption			**Government corruption**	
	#	%		#	%
Government effectiveness	577	49.9%	Government effectiveness	5,433	48.1%
Voice and accountability	177	15.3%	Voice and accountability	1,530	13.5%
Regulatory quality	124	10.7%	Regulatory quality	1,132	10.0%
Political stability	38	3.3%	Political stability	544	4.8%
Rule of law	36	3.1%	Rule of law	440	3.9%
Control of corruption	15	1.3%	Control of corruption	175	1.5%
Unknown	190	16.4%	Unknown	2,052	18.1%
	Government effectiveness			**Government effectiveness**	
Government effectiveness	337	46.6%	Government effectiveness	5,672	48.3%
Voice and accountability	109	15.1%	Voice and accountability	1,598	13.6%
Regulatory quality	78	10.8%	Regulatory quality	1,178	10.0%
Political stability	28	3.9%	Political stability	448	3.8%
Rule of law	26	3.6%	Rule of law	556	4.7%
Control of corruption	8	1.1%	Control of corruption	182	1.6%
Unknown	137	18.9%	Unknown	2,105	17.9%
	Political stability			**Political stability**	
Government effectiveness	1,448	51.8%	Government effectiveness	4,562	47.2%
Voice and accountability	374	13.4%	Voice and accountability	1,333	13.8%
Regulatory quality	265	9.5%	Regulatory quality	991	10.3%

Table 28 (cont.)

	Political stability			Political stability	
Rule of law	123	4.4%	Rule of law	458	4.7%
Political stability	95	3.4%	Political stability	381	3.9%
Control of corruption	41	1.5%	Control of corruption	149	1.5%
Unknown	451	16.1%	Unknown	1,791	18.5%

	Regulatory quality			Regulatory quality	
Government effectiveness	450	48.4%	Government effectiveness	5,317	47.1%
Voice and accountability	143	15.4%	Voice and accountability	1,561	13.8%
Regulatory quality	97	10.4%	Regulatory quality	1,158	10.3%
Political stability	31	3.3%	Political stability	444	3.9%
Rule of law	28	3.0%	Rule of law	552	4.9%
Control of corruption	12	1.3%	Control of corruption	178	1.6%
Unknown	169	18.2%	Unknown	2,069	18.3%

	Rule of law			Rule of law	
Government effectiveness	329	46.2%	Government effectiveness	5,429	47.2%
Voice and accountability	110	15.4%	Voice and accountability	1,598	13.9%
Regulatory quality	76	10.7%	Regulatory quality	1,180	10.3%
Political stability	27	3.8%	Political stability	449	3.9%
Rule of law	24	3.4%	Rule of law	558	4.9%
Control of corruption	8	1.1%	Control of corruption	182	1.6%
Unknown	138	19.4%	Unknown	2,104	18.3%

Table 28 (cont.)

	Voice and accountability			Voice and accountability	
Government effectiveness	671	48.4%	Government effectiveness	5,087	47.0%
Voice and accountability	199	14.4%	Voice and accountability	1,509	13.9%
Regulatory quality	148	10.7%	Regulatory quality	1,108	10.2%
Rule of law	52	3.8%	Rule of law	530	4.9%
Political stability	39	2.8%	Political stability	437	4.0%
Control of corruption	25	1.8%	Control of corruption	165	1.5%
Unknown	252	18.2%	Unknown	1,990	18.4%

indicator, scholars in lower-scoring countries prioritised research on local government (1.5% higher TW than in high-scoring countries), performance management (0.5% higher TW than in high-scoring countries), networks (0.3% higher TW than in high-scoring countries) and federal government (0.2% higher TW than in high-scoring countries). Government finances (finance/budgeting) were only a top five topic in low-scoring countries, and people management (HRM) was only a top five topic in high-scoring countries.

Differences of over 1% in topic weights were also observed for the voice and accountability and political stability indicators. In the political stability indicator category, scholars in high-scoring countries focused on three topics: security, risk management and conflict management. In contrast, scholars in low-scoring countries placed more emphasis on accountability (0.9% higher TW), representative bureaucracy (0.8% higher TW), transparency (0.7% higher TW) and citizen participation (0.6% higher TW), suggesting that scholars working in countries that score low on government corruption examine voice and accountability and the effectiveness of government to a greater extent than those in high-scoring countries, with perhaps a focus on improving the quality of government.

In the high-scoring subsample, topic weights in the government effectiveness indicator were higher for government effectiveness (1.7% higher TW) and for rule of law (1.1% higher TW) than in the low-scoring countries. There was a stronger focus on voice and accountability (1.5% higher TW) in the low-scoring subsample than in the high-scoring subsample. While scholars in high-scoring countries dedicated more attention to government effectiveness, the highest topic weights in the low-scoring subsample were associated with federal government (4.7% vs. 3.9%) and local government (3.7% versus 2.5%), suggesting a focus on structures.

In contrast, scholars in high-scoring countries placed more emphasis on performance management (3.9% versus 2.8%) and included HRM in the top five topics, implying a stronger interest in questions of management. There were no substantial differences between the two subsamples in the prominence of different governance dimensions associated with regulatory quality, political stability and control of corruption.

The political stability indicator showed the least variation between low- and high-scoring countries, with negligible differences across the topic weights, with one exception. The gap in the topic weights between low- and high-scoring countries was largest for the government effectiveness indicator, at 4.6%. An emphasis on structures was again seen in the low-scoring subsample: federal government (TW of 4.1% versus 3.5%) and local government. It was not even a top five topic for high-scoring countries. In addition, two management topics were present in the top five topics in low-scoring countries – HRM and performance management – but they had lower topic weights than in high-scoring countries. The networks topic was more prominent in high-scoring countries (TW of 3.5% versus 2.65%). These findings again point towards interest in research questions on government structure in low-scoring countries.

When we compared the distribution of topics related to the regulatory quality indicator, we found that government effectiveness (1.3% higher TW) and voice and accountability (1.6% higher TW) had higher topic weights in high-scoring countries than in low-scoring countries, and the opposite pattern for the rule of law (1.9% higher TW). Within the government effectiveness indicator, structures was again more common in low-scoring countries: federal government had a 0.7% higher topic weight in low-scoring countries than in high-scoring countries, and there was a 0.4% higher topic weight for both local government and networks. Management was also featured in low-scoring countries, with performance management having a 0.1% higher topic weight than in high-scoring countries. High-scoring countries also conducted more research on the topic of HRM.

For the rule of law, two governance indicators presented differences in topic weights of over 1%: government effectiveness was 1% higher in high-scoring countries and voice and accountability was 1.5% higher in low-scoring countries. Government effectiveness was the most prominent governance dimension discussed in both subsamples, followed by voice and accountability, regulatory quality, political stability and rule of law. Within government effectiveness, the emphasis on structures was again seen in low-scoring countries: topic weights were higher for local government (1.4%), federal government (0.8%) and networks (0.4%). Topic weights were higher for performance measurement in high-scoring countries (0.4%). PSM and red tape was a top five topic in low-scoring countries and HRM was one in high-scoring countries. For the voice and accountability indicator, low-scoring countries conducted more research than high-scoring countries on accountability (1.1% higher TW), representative bureaucracy (1% higher TW) and citizen participation (0.1% higher TW) but less on transparency (0.1% higher TW). User choice was among the top five topics in low-scoring countries only, whereas gender and diversity was only included in the top five topics in high-scoring countries.

For the final World Bank Governance Indicator, voice and accountability, differences of over 1% in topic weights were seen for government effectiveness (1.4% higher TW in low-scoring countries) and rule of law (1.1% higher TW in high-scoring countries). The focus on government structures was again higher in low-scoring countries: local government (1.1% higher TW) and networks (0.3% higher TW). However, scholars in high-scoring countries examined federal government more frequently (0.2% higher TW). Scholars in low-scoring countries focused on performance measurement slightly more than those in high-scoring countries (0.2% higher TW). PSM and red tape was among the top five topics by weight in low-scoring countries and HRM was a top five topic in high-scoring countries.

The variations in topic weights given to World Bank Governance Indicators across the groups were not large. However, there were important differences in the research agendas of countries/regions with low and high governance scores. In countries/regions that score relatively low on these indicators, there is often an emphasis on research that examines the structures of government, whereas in countries/regions with high governance scores, scholarship is geared more towards questions of management.

6 Conclusions

The purpose of this Element was to extend the academic debate on the nature of the public administration discipline by better understanding how it has developed and its current trajectories. This aim is related to scholarship that has examined the theoretical foundations of the discipline from a number of perspectives (Ferlie et al. 2005; Frederickson et al. 2016; Peters and Pierre 2003; Rosenbloom et al. 1993). However, rather than adopting the deductive methodologies often seen in such reviews, we applied a novel methodology that has rarely been used in public administration. The results show the potential of computational social sciences (Walker et al. 2019, 2023) and corpus linguistics (Chandra 2016b; Gries 2009; McEnery and Hardy 2012) for the discipline. Public administration has often borrowed methodologies from other disciplines to advance the field – a notable recent example is the now widespread use of experimental methods (James et al. 2017) – and this is a prime example of how new insights can be obtained through methodological innovation.

In the first part of our study, we analysed our stock of 12,760 academic articles published in seventeen journals between 1991 and 2019 and identified the top fifty topics in public administration. This highlighted many topics that scholars of public administration would recognise as core to the discipline: federal government, performance management, HRM, networks, citizen participation, transparency to list six of the top ten topics. Other prominent topics were policy arenas, including health care, science policy, labour/employment policy, education, economic policy and family policy. Articles focused on questions of policy processes and policy implementation were not very common in our corpus, perhaps because such topics were the context for studies of the processes and consequence of public administration and public service delivery. As we note below in our discussion of limitations, other linguistics techniques such as collocation analysis could provide more nuanced insight into the topics, helping us to understand the context in which they are used and thus better understand their meaning.

Our analysis enabled us to quantify the stock of topics of public administration between 1991 and 2019 and draw the following conclusions:

- A total of 80% of scholarship in public administration focused on core questions of administration/management, policy and structures. Twenty of the fifty topics examined questions of administration and management (TW = 40.4%) followed by policy (eleven topics; TW = 21.4%) and structures and process of governance (ten topics; TW = 18.7).
- Just over one-third of scholarship in public administration during our sample period was dedicated to ten topics: health care, federal government, performance management, environmental regulation, HRM, networks, citizen participation, transparency, science policy and local government.
- Topics related to concepts (e.g., neoliberalism), accountability or the law were in the minority. The topics of public service motivation and red tape have been developed and honed in the public administration literature. These two topics were associated by probability with each other in one topic and ranked twenty-ninth out of the fifty topics in public administration.

By applying computational social science techniques to individual journals, we were able to examine and contrast our inductively developed topics with the aims and scopes of seventeen public administration journals. There was often a strong correlation between the journal aims and scopes and our topics, which highlighted the unique focuses of the journals in the field. However, not all of the published topics aligned with the journals' stated scopes, objectives and aims. For example, *EPC* has changed its focus from government and policy to politics and space, and the analysis of the change in topics over the study period captured key aspects of the journal's and field's historical priorities.

Our analysis provides important insights into the distribution of topics across journals, with the seven topics figuring in at least five journals: networks (included in nine journals), gender and diversity (in seven journals), health care (in seven journals), partnerships (in six journals), HRM (in five journals), finance and budgeting (in five journals) and privatisation (in five journals). Furthermore, these seven topics were found in all of the journals in our corpus. This suggests that these topics form the core topics of the public administration field, when journals are used as the unit of analysis. A possible use for the analysis of topics within journals could be to assist scholars in making decisions about where to submit their manuscripts.

In Table 29, we compare the findings from stock of the two corpora: the top seven journal topic rankings and the ranking of those topics in the fifty public administration topics identified for the whole corpus. We find the following variation in rank order: (a) three topics – networks (ranked sixth, TW = 3.0%), health care (ranked first, TW = 4.1%), HRM (ranked fifth, TW = 3.0%) – are among the top ten topics across all journals, (b) the two topics of partnership (ranked fifteenth, TW = 2.2%) and privatisation (twelfth, TW= 2.4%) are ranked between eleven and twenty in all topic lists and (c) two of the top seven journal topics – gender and diversity (ranked twenty-first, TW = 2.0%) and finance and budgeting (ranked twenty-third, TW = 2.0%) – are in the top twenty of the fifty topics. This reinforces the different priorities of the individual journals relative to the priorities of the whole corpus, and points towards

Table 29 Comparing the ranking of the most popular topics in journals and across all journals

Topic	Ranking among the most popular seven topics in individual journals	Ranking in the fifty topics of public administration
Networks	1	6
Gender and diversity	2	21
Health care	3	1
Partnerships	4	15
HRM	5	5
Finance and budgeting	6	22
Privatization	7	12

important topics of scholarship in the public administration discipline. Notably, the topics of health care, networks and HRM figured prominently in each of these corpora.

Moving to our analysis of the flow of topics over time, the corpus linguistics methodology of keyness showed stark differences in the keywords in the early and later periods of the study period.

- Examination of the keywords in the early period (1991–1995) in the stock of all journals and within the analysis of individual journals saw two words mentioned more than two times across each of these corpora. This included Britain/British and health/medicine/NHS.
- Looking at the later period (2015–2019), five keywords were mentioned on more than two occasions and in each corpus. These were governance, collaboration/coordination, citizens, networks and actors.

The change of keywords from the early to the late period are suggestive of a flow of scholarship away from perhaps more practice-orientated scholarship in public administration towards the analysis of concepts. This would be in keeping with Pollitt's (2017) 'managerialization' thesis in which he argued that public administration scholarship became more academic, with emphasis placed on conceptual measurement and methodological sophistication at the expense of real-world problems. This thesis was recently given validity in an analysis of academic and practice literature using the computational and linguistic techniques adopted in this study (Walker et al. 2023).

Contrasting the keywords from the later period in the analysis over time and the top topics identified in the journals (Table 19), a relationship of keywords and topics is apparent. The clearest matches to terms were the keywords collaboration and the topics of collaboration and partnership, and networks and networks. The two keywords governance and citizens were included in the citizen participation and regional governance and multilevel governance topics from the full corpus, while the two keywords employees and municipalities were associated with the topics HRM and local government. However, it is possible that the relatively limited number and scope of the keywords in the early period was a function of the small sample, which contained fewer journals and articles than the late period sample.

To examine the flow of individual topics over time we plotted changing topic weights. Of the top ten topics (Figure 1), the flow of the topic weights of six topics was upwards – federal government, performance management, environmental regulation, HRM, science policy and local government. The balance of topics weights was relatively flat over time for three topics – networks, citizen participation and transparency. That three topics had relatively flat topics weights over time speaks to their enduring importance in the field, and importantly the two topics of networks and citizens occur frequently in our various analysis, for example topics in journals and keyness analysis. It is also interesting to note that the most written about topic – health care – was highlighted in the early time period keyness analysis yet has seen one of the most precipitous declines of any topic over time, falling from around 15% of all scholarship in 1991 to around 2.5% by 2019.

In our analysis of the distribution of topics and their geography, we divided the sample according to countries' scores on the World Bank Governance Indicators and identified a clear rank order of indicators based on the number of topics associated with each indicator: government effectiveness, voice and accountability, regulatory quality, rule of law, political stability and control of corruption. The country analysis highlighted (a) as may be expected, much higher levels of scholarship in countries associated with high scores on the governance indicators and (b) a pattern in the two indicators associated with the highest number of topics. For government effectiveness, scholars in low-scoring countries typically examined questions of structure – federal government, local government and networks – whereas scholars in high-scoring countries prioritised management questions, such as HRM and performance management. For the voice and accountability indicator, scholars in low-scoring countries placed more emphasis on accountability, citizen participation and representative bureaucracy. It is, however, important to recognise that the balance of the scholarship is found in the countries associated with high scores in the World Bank Governance Indicators, where around 90% of the articles were published. Overall, we developed a novel approach to examining geographical variations in the topics of public administration that highlights important variations in the focus of scholarship in different contexts. Specifically, we found in countries with:

- Weaker scores on the World Bank Governance Indicators a focus on structures of government, and
- Stronger scores on the World Bank Governance Indicators a focus on management and governance.

Our study has a number of limitations that need to be considered when interpreting the findings. Using a different corpus, for example all journals from a single index or over different time spans – going back further in time (although there would be problems of comprehensive digital data) or forward to capture more recent publications – is likely to result in different topic lists as the field of public administration is continually evolving. Similarly, our approach to capturing the geography of public administration could be enhanced and further developed to capture more subtle variations between countries, regions or cultures.

Computational social sciences and corpus linguistics have great potential to systematically integrate studies and advance knowledge in the field of public administration. They can be applied to a range of questions about the development of the field. Future research could use collocation analysis to further examine the relevance of academic research to practice using the corpora from this project. For example, health care, contracting, strategic planning and budgeting were four common topics in our corpus. Collocation analysis could be used to delve further into these topics and how they are examined in academia. We encourage others to explore these methodologies from computational social sciences and linguistics to further develop understanding of the discipline of public administration.

Appendix

Table A1 Comparison of topics between countries scoring low
and high in control of corruption

	Countries scoring low			Countries scoring high	
	#	%		#	%
Control of corruption					
urban governance	15	1.3%	urban governance	175	1.5%
Government effectiveness					
performance management	50	4.3%	federal government	443	3.9%
federal government	47	4.1%	performance management	427	3.8%
local government	45	3.9%	HRM	361	3.2%
networks	38	3.3%	networks	335	3.0%
finance/budgeting	30	2.6%	local government	274	2.4%
Political security					
security	16	1.4%	security	197	1.7%
risk management	10	0.9%	risk management	127	1.1%
conflict management	10	0.9%	conflict management	116	1.0%
Regulatory quality					
environmental regulation	35	3.0%	environmental regulation	347	3.1%
contracting	34	2.9%	welfare regimes	277	2.5%
welfare regimes	28	2.4%	privatization	266	2.4%
privatization	27	2.3%	contracting	242	2.1%
Rule of law					
economic policy	16	1.4%	labor/employment policy	252	2.2%
labor/employment policy	15	1.3%	economic policy	176	1.6%
procedural justice	7	0.6%	procedural justice	116	1.0%
Voice and accountability					
citizen participation	38	3.3%	citizen participation	302	2.7%
transparency	35	3.0%	transparency	300	2.7%
representative bureaucracy	33	2.9%	representative bureaucracy	241	2.1%

Table A1 (cont.)

	Countries scoring low			Countries scoring high	
	#	%		#	%
accountability	28	2.4%	gender and diversity	236	2.1%
user choice	16	1.4%	accountability	171	1.5%
Unknown					
health care	42	3.6%	health care	459	4.1%
development aid	37	3.2%	science policy	317	2.8%
nonprofits	20	1.7%	nonprofits	216	1.9%
education	20	1.7%	development aid	206	1.8%
science policy	19	1.6%	europe	194	1.7%

Table A2 Comparison of topics between countries scoring low and high in government effectiveness

	Countries scoring low			Countries scoring high	
	#	%		#	%
Control of corruption					
urban governance	8	1.1%	urban governance	182	1.6%
Government effectiveness					
federal government	34	4.7%	federal government	456	3.9%
local government	27	3.7%	performance management	456	3.9%
networks	24	3.3%	HRM	371	3.2%
performance management	20	2.8%	networks	349	3.0%
PSM and red tape	18	2.5%	local government	292	2.5%
Political stability					
security	13	1.8%	security	200	1.7%
risk management	9	1.2%	risk management	128	1.1%
conflict management	6	0.8%	conflict management	120	1.0%
Regulatory quality					
welfare regimes	24	3.3%	environmental regulation	362	3.1%
environmental regulation	20	2.8%	welfare regimes	281	2.4%
privatization	18	2.5%	privatization	275	2.3%
contracting	16	2.2%	contracting	260	2.2%

Table A2 (cont.)

	Countries scoring low			Countries scoring high	
	#	%		#	%
Rule of law					
labor/employment policy	11	1.5%	labor/employment policy	256	2.2%
economic policy	10	1.4%	economic policy	182	1.6%
procedural justice	5	0.7%	procedural justice	118	1.0%
Voice and accountability					
citizen participation	21	2.9%	citizen participation	319	2.7%
representative bureaucracy	21	2.9%	transparency	316	2.7%
accountability	19	2.6%	representative bureaucracy	253	2.2%
transparency	18	2.5%	gender and diversity	242	2.1%
user choice	11	1.5%	accountability	180	1.5%
Unknown					
health care	38	5.3%	health care	463	3.9%
development aid	32	4.4%	science policy	327	2.8%
family policy	13	1.8%	nonprofits	224	1.9%
nonprofits	12	1.7%	development aid	211	1.8%
education	10	1.4%	europe	197	1.7%

Table A3 Comparison of topics between countries scoring low and high in political stability

	Countries scoring low			Countries scoring high	
	#	%		#	%
Control of corruption					
urban governance	149	1.5%	urban governance	41	1.5%
Government effectiveness					
federal government	392	4.1%	HRM	142	5.1%
performance management	368	3.8%	performance management	109	3.9%
networks	274	2.8%	networks	99	3.5%

Table A3 (cont.)

	Countries scoring low			Countries scoring high	
	#	%		#	%
local government	252	2.6%	federal government	98	3.5%
HRM	239	2.5%	collaboration	90	3.2%
Political stability					
security	182	1.9%	risk management	35	1.3%
risk management	102	1.1%	security	31	1.1%
conflict management	97	1.0%	conflict management	29	1.0%
Regulatory quality					
environmental regulation	284	2.9%	environmental regulation	98	3.5%
welfare regimes	254	2.6%	contracting	62	2.2%
privatization	239	2.5%	privatization	54	1.9%
contracting	214	2.2%	welfare regimes	51	1.8%
Rule of law					
labor/employment policy	207	2.1%	labor/ employment policy	59	2.1%
economic policy	153	1.6%	economic policy	39	1.4%
procedural justice	98	1.0%	procedural justice	25	0.9%
Voice and accountability					
transparency	256	2.6%	citizen participation	87	3.1%
citizen participation	253	2.6%	transparency	78	2.8%
representative bureaucracy	211	2.2%	representative bureaucracy	63	2.3%
gender and diversity	195	2.0%	gender and diversity	56	2.0%
accountability	157	1.6%	accountability	42	1.5%
Unknown					
health care	410	4.2%	health care	91	3.3%
science policy	272	2.8%	nonprofits	66	2.4%
development aid	204	2.1%	science policy	64	2.3%
nonprofits	170	1.8%	education	62	2.2%
europe	170	1.8%	development aid	39	1.4%

Table A4 Comparison of topics between countries scoring low
and high in regulatory quality

	Countries scoring low			Countries scoring high	
	#	%		#	%
Control of corruption			**Control of corruption**		
urban governance	12	1.3%	urban governance	178	1.6%
government effectiveness		0.0%			0.0%
federal government	44	4.7%	federal government	446	4.0%
performance management	37	4.0%	performance management	439	3.9%
networks	32	3.4%	HRM	365	3.2%
local government	32	3.4%	networks	340	3.0%
collaboration	26	2.8%	local government	287	2.5%
Political stability		0.0%			0.0%
security	14	1.5%	security	199	1.8%
risk management	9	1.0%	risk management	128	1.1%
conflict management	8	0.9%	conflict management	117	1.0%
Regulatory quality		0.0%			0.0%
contracting	27	2.9%	environmental regulation	356	3.2%
environmental regulation	26	2.8%	welfare regimes	279	2.5%
welfare regimes	26	2.8%	privatization	274	2.4%
privatization	18	1.9%	contracting	249	2.2%
Rule of law		0.0%			0.0%
labour/employment policy	14	1.5%	labour/employment policy	252	2.2%
economic policy	11	1.2%	economic policy	180	1.6%
procedural justice	3	0.3%	procedural justice	120	1.1%
Voice and accountability		0.0%			0.0%
transparency	30	3.2%	citizen participation	313	2.8%
citizen participation	27	2.9%	transparency	305	2.7%
representative bureaucracy	26	2.8%	representative bureaucracy	248	2.2%
accountability	25	2.7%	gender and diversity	235	2.1%
user choice	13	1.4%	accountability	174	1.5%
gender and diversity	13	1.4%			0.0%
Unknown		0.0%			0.0%
health care	38	4.1%	health care	461	4.1%
development aid	36	3.9%	science policy	320	2.8%
education	19	2.0%	nonprofits	218	1.9%
nonprofits	18	1.9%	development aid	207	1.8%
science policy	16	1.7%	europe	197	1.7%
family policy	16	1.7%			0.0%

Table A5 Comparison of topics between countries scoring low
and high in rule of law

	Countries scoring low			Countries scoring high	
	#	%		#	%
Control of corruption			**Control of corruption**		
urban governance	8	1.1%	urban governance	182	1.6%
Government effectiveness					
federal government	34	4.8%	federal government	456	4.0%
local government	28	3.9%	performance management	452	3.9%
performance management	25	3.5%	HRM	371	3.2%
networks	24	3.4%	networks	349	3.0%
PSM and red tape	19	2.7%	local government	291	2.5%
Political stability					
security	12	1.7%	security	201	1.7%
risk management	9	1.3%	risk management	128	1.1%
conflict management	6	0.8%	conflict management	120	1.0%
Regulatory quality					
welfare regimes	24	3.4%	environmental regulation	362	3.1%
environmental regulation	20	2.8%	welfare regimes	281	2.4%
privatization	16	2.2%	privatization	277	2.4%
contracting	16	2.2%	contracting	260	2.3%
Rule of law					
labour/employment policy	12	1.7%	labour/employment policy	255	2.2%
economic policy	9	1.3%	economic policy	183	1.6%
procedural justice	3	0.4%	procedural justice	120	1.0%
Voice and accountability					
representative bureaucracy	22	3.1%	citizen participation	319	2.8%
citizen participation	21	2.9%	transparency	317	2.8%
transparency	18	2.5%	representative bureaucracy	252	2.2%
accountability	18	2.5%	gender and diversity	241	2.1%
user choice	11	1.5%	accountability	181	1.6%
Unknown					
health care	36	5.1%	health care	465	4.0%
development aid	34	4.8%	science policy	326	2.8%
family policy	14	2.0%	nonprofits	224	1.9%
nonprofits	12	1.7%	development aid	209	1.8%
science policy	10	1.4%	europe	198	1.7%
education	10	1.4%	education	196	1.7%

Table A6 Comparison of topics between countries scoring low
and high in voice and accountability

	Countries scoring low			Countries scoring high	
	#	%		#	%
Control of corruption			**Control of corruption**		
urban governance	25	1.8%	urban governance	165	1.5%
Government effectiveness					
performance management	57	4.1%	federal government	437	4.0%
federal government	53	3.8%	performance management	420	3.9%
local government	50	3.6%	HRM	349	3.2%
networks	46	3.3%	networks	327	3.0%
PSM and red tape	38	2.7%	local government	269	2.5%
Political stability					
security	19	1.4%	security	194	1.8%
risk management	12	0.9%	risk management	125	1.2%
conflict management	8	0.6%	conflict management	118	1.1%
Regulatory quality					
environmental regulation	49	3.5%	environmental regulation	333	3.1%
contracting	35	2.5%	welfare regimes	272	2.5%
welfare regimes	33	2.4%	privatization	262	2.4%
privatization	31	2.2%	contracting	241	2.2%
Rule of law					
economic policy	21	1.5%	labour/employment policy	248	2.3%
labour/employment policy	19	1.4%	economic policy	171	1.6%
procedural justice	12	0.9%	procedural justice	111	1.0%
Voice and accountability					
citizen participation	44	3.2%	transparency	297	2.7%
transparency	38	2.7%	citizen participation	296	2.7%
representative bureaucracy	34	2.5%	representative bureaucracy	240	2.2%
accountability	33	2.4%	gender and diversity	231	2.1%
gender and diversity	20	1.4%	accountability	166	1.5%
Development					
health care	53	3.8%	health care	448	4.1%
development aid	45	3.2%	science policy	307	2.8%
science policy	29	2.1%	nonprofits	208	1.9%
nonprofits	28	2.0%	development aid	198	1.8%
education	26	1.9%	europe	190	1.8%

References

Andrews, R. & Esteve, M. (2015). Still like ships that pass in the night? The relationship between public administration and management studies. *International public management journal*, 18(1), 31–60.

Baker, P. & McEnery, M. A. (2005). A corpus-based approach to discourses of refugees and asylum seekers in UN and newspaper texts. *Journal of language and politics*, 4(2), 197–226.

Bennett, A. (2015). Found in translation: Combining discourse analysis with computer assisted content analysis. *Millennium*, 43, 984–997.

Blei, D. M. (2012). Probabilistic topic models. *Communications of the ACM*, 55(4), 77–84.

Blei, D. M. & Jordan, M. I. (2003, July). Modeling annotated data. In *Proceedings of the 26th annual international ACM SIGIR conference on research and development in information retrieval* (pp. 127–134).

Blei, D. M. & Lafferty, J. D. (2007). A correlated topic model of science. *The annals of applied statistics*, 1(1), 17–35.

Bohne, E., Graham, J. D. & Raadschelders, J. C. N. (2014). *Public Administration and the Modern State*. London: Palgrave Macmillan.

Chandra, Y. (2016a). Social entrepreneurship as institutional-change work: A corpus linguistics analysis. *Journal of social entrepreneurship*, 8(1), 14–46. https://doi.org/10.1080/19420676.2016.1233133.

Chandra, Y. (2016b). A rhetoric-orientation view of social entrepreneurship. *Social enterprise journal*, 12(2), 161–200.

Chandra, Y., Jiang, L. C. & Wang, C.-J. (2016). Mining social entrepreneurship strategies using topic modeling. *PLoS One*, 11(3), e0151342.

Chandra, Y. & Shang, C. (2019). *Qualitative Research Using R: A Systematic Approach*. Singapore: Springer.

Chandra, Y. & Walker, R. M. (2018). How does a seminal article in public administration diffuse and influence the field? Bibliometric methods and the case of Hood's 'A public management for all seasons'. *International public management journal*, 22(5), 712–742.

Corley, E. A. & Sabharwal, M. (2010). Scholarly collaboration and productivity patterns in public administration: Analyzing recent trends. *Public administration*, 88(4), 627–648.

Cox III, R. W., Buck, S. J. & Morgan, B. N. (2016). *Public Administration in Theory and Practice*. New York: Routledge.

Curry, D. & Van de Walle, S. (2016). A bibliometrics approach to understanding conceptual breadth, depth and development: The case of new public management. *Political studies review*, 26(2), 113–124.

De Vries, H., Bekkers, V. & Tummers, L. (2016). Innovation in the public sector: A systematic review and research agenda. *Public administration*, 94(1), 146–166.

Ding, F., Lu, J. & Riccucci, N. M. (2021). How bureaucratic representation affects public organizational performance: A meta-analysis. *Public administration review*, 81(6), 1003–1018.

Ennser-Jedenastik, L. & Meyer, T. M. (2018). The impact of party cues on manual coding of political texts. *Political science research & methods*, 6(3), 625–633.

Fairclough, N. (2013). Critical discourse analysis and critical policy studies. *Critical policy studies*, 7(2), 177–197.

Feinerer, I. (2015). Introduction to the tm package text mining in R. 2013-12-01. www.dainf.ct.utfpr.edu.br/~kaestner/Mineracao/RDataMining/tm.pdf.

Ferlie, E., Lynn Jr., L. E. & Pollitt, C. (2005). *The Oxford Handbook of Public Management*. Oxford: Oxford University Press.

Frederickson, H. G., Smith, K. B., Larimer, C. W. & Licari, M. (2016). *The Public Administration Theory Primer*. Boulder, CO: Westview Press.

George, B., Andersen, L. B., Hall, J. L. & Pandey, S. K. (2023). Writing impactful reviews to rejuvenate public administration: A framework and recommendations. *Public administration review*, 83(6), 1517–1527.

George, B., Pandey, S. K., Steijn, B., Decramer, A. & Audenaert, M. (2021). Red tape, organizational performance, and employee outcomes: Meta-analysis, meta-regression and research agenda. *Public administration review*, 81(4), 810–819.

George, B., Walker, R. M. & Monster, J. (2019). Does strategic planning improve organizational performance? A meta-analysis. *Public administration review*, 79(6), 810–819.

Gerrish, E. (2016). The impact of performance management on performance in public organizations: A meta-analysis. *Public administration review*, 76(1), 48–66.

Gries, S. T. (2009). What is corpus linguistics? *Language and linguistics compass*, 3(5), 1225–1241.

Gries, S. T. (2016). *Quantitative Corpus Linguistics with R: A Practical Introduction*. London: Taylor & Francis.

Grün, B. & Hornik, K. (2011). Topicmodels: An R package for fitting topic models. *Journal of statistical software*, 40(13), 1–30.

Gulrajani, N. & Moloney, K. (2012). Globalizing public administration: Today's research and tomorrow's agenda. *Public administration review*, 72(1), 78–86.

Hattke, F. & Vogel, R. (2023). Theories and theorizing in public administration: A systematic review. *Public administration review*, 83(6), 1542–1563.

Hollibaugh Jr., G. E. (2019). The use of text as data methods in public administration: A review and an application to agency priorities. *Journal of public administration research and theory*, 29(3), 474–490.

Hornik, K. & Grün, B. (2011). Topicmodels: An R package for fitting topic models. *Journal of statistical software*, 40(13), 1–30.

James, O., Jilke, S. R. & Van Ryzin, G. G. (2017). *Experiments in Public Management Research*: *Challenges and Contributions*. Cambridge: Cambridge University Press.

Kaplan, S. & Vakili, K. (2014). The double-edged sword of recombination in breakthrough innovation. *Strategic management journal*, 36(10), 1435–1457.

Kaufmann, W. & Haans R. F. J. (2021). Understanding the meaning of concepts across domains through collocation analysis: An application to the study of red tape. *Journal of public administration research and theory*, 31(1), 218–233.

Krippendorff, K. (2004). Reliability in content analysis: Some common misconceptions and recommendations. *Human communication research*, 30(3), 411–433.

Landauer, T. K., McNamara, D. S., Dennis, S. & Kintsch W. (Eds.) (2013). *Handbook of Latent Semantic Analysis*. New York: Routledge.

L'Hôte, E. (2010). New labour and globalization: Globalist discourse with a twist? *Discourse & society*, 21(2), 355–376.

Li, H. & Zhang, J. (2021). Chinese public administration research in mainstream PA journals: A systematic review (2002–20). In Bryer, T. A. Ed. *Handbook of Theories of Public Administration and Management*, 286–298, Cheltenham: Edward Elgar.

Li, Y., Chandra, Y. & Fan, Y. (2022). Unpacking government social media messaging strategies during the COVID-19 pandemic in China. *Policy & internet*, 14(3), 651–672.

McEnery, T. & Hardie, A. (2012). *Corpus Linguistics*: *Method, Theory and Practice*. Cambridge: Cambridge University Press.

Meier, K. J. & O'Toole Jr., L. J. (2003a). Public management and educational performance: The impact of managerial networking. *Public administration review*, 63(6), 698–699.

Meier, K. J. & O'Toole Jr., L. J. (2003b). Plus ca change: Public management, personnel stability, and organizational performance. *Journal of public administration research and theory*, 13(1), 43–64.

Norris, N. (1997). Error, bias and validity in qualitative research. *Educational action research*, 5(1), 172–176.

O'Reilly, D. & Reed, M. (2011). The grit in the oyster: Professionalism, managerialism and leaderism as discourses of UK public services modernization. *Organization studies*, 32(8), 1079–1101.

Pandey, S., Pandey, S. K. & Miller, L. (2017). Measuring innovativeness of public organizations: Using natural language processing techniques in computer-aided textual analysis. *International public management journal*, 20(1), 78–107.

Parkinson, C. & Howorth, C. (2008). The language of social entrepreneurs. *Entrepreneurship & regional development*, 20(3), 285–309.

Pastrana, T., Jünger, S., Ostgathe, C., Elsner, F. & Radbruch, L. (2008). A matter of definition – key elements identified in a discourse analysis of definitions of palliative care. *Palliative medicine*, 22(3), 222–232.

Paul, M. J. & Dredze, M. (2014). Discovering health topics in social media using topic models. *PLoS One*, 9(8), e103408.

Perren, L. & Sapsed, J. (2013). Innovation as politics: The rise and reshaping of innovation in UK parliamentary discourse 1960–2005. *Research policy*, 42(10), 1815–1828.

Perry, J. L. (2012). How can we improve our science to generate more usable knowledge for public professionals? *Public administration review*, 72(3), 479–482.

Peters, B. G. & Pierre, J. (2003). *Handbook of Public Administration*. Thousand Oaks, CA: Sage.

Pollitt, C. (2017). Public administration research since 1980: Slipping away from the real world. *International journal of public sector management*, 30 (6/7), 555–565.

Pollitt, C. & Bouckaert, G. (2004). *Public Management Reform: A Comparative Analysis*. Oxford: Oxford University Press.

Prior, L., Hughes, D. & Peckham, S. (2012). The discursive turn in policy analysis and the validation of policy stories. *Journal of social policy*, 41(2), 271–289.

Quinn, K. M., Monroe, B. L., Colaresi, M., Crespin, M. H. & Radev D. R. (2010). How to analyze political attention with minimal assumptions and costs. *American journal of political science*, 54(1), 209–228.

Raadschelders, J. C. N. (2011). *Public Administration: The Interdisciplinary Study of Government*. Oxford: Oxford University Press.

Raadschelders, J. C. N. & Vigoda-Gadot, E. (2015). *Global Dimensions of Public Administration and Governance: Comparative Perspectives*. San Francisco, CA: Jossey Bass.

Rayson, P. (2008). From key words to key semantic domains. *International journal of corpus linguistics*, 13(4), 519–549.

Rheault, L. & Cochrane, C. (2020). Word embeddings for the analysis of ideological placement in parliamentary corpora. *Political analysis*, 28(1), 112–113.

Ritz, A., Brewer, G. A. & Neumann, O. (2016). Public service motivation: A systematic literature review and outlook. *Public administration review*, 76(3), 414–426.

Rosenbloom, D. H., Goldman, D. D. & Wayne, S. (1993). *Public Administration: Understanding Management, Politics, and Law in the Public Sector*. New York: McGraw-Hill.

Rosenthal, R. (1991). *Meta-Analytical Procedures for Social Science*. London: Sage.

Scott, M. (2008). *WordSmith tools version 5*. Liverpool: Lexical Analysis Software, 122.

Simon, H. (1996). *Sciences of the Artificial*. 3rd Ed. Cambridge, MA: MIT Press.

Tirunillai, S. & Tellis, G. J. (2014). Mining marketing meaning from online chatter: Strategic brand analysis of big data using latent dirichlet allocation. *Journal of marketing research*, 51(4), 463–479.

Van de Walle, S. & van Delft, R. (2015). Publishing in public administration: Issues with defining, comparing and ranking the output of universities. *International public management journal*, 18(1), 87–107.

Vogel, R. (2014). What happened to the public organization? A bibliometric analysis of public administration and organization studies. *The American review of public administration*, 44(4), 383–408.

Vogel, R. & Hatte, F. (2022). A century of public administration: Traveling through time and topics. *Public administration*, 100(1), 17–40.

Walker, R. M. (2014a). Guest editor: Public administration in east and southeast Asia: A review of the evidence. *American review of public administration*, 44(2), 131–209.

Walker, R. M. (2014b). Internal and external antecedents of process innovation in local government: A review and extension. *Public management review*, 16(1), 21–44.

Walker, R. M. & Andrews, R. (2015). Local government management and performance: A review of evidence. *Journal of public administration research and theory*, 25(1), 101–133.

Walker, R. M., Chandra, Y., Zhang, J. & van Witteloosijin, A. (2019). Topic modeling the research-practice gap in public administration. *Public administration review*, 79(6), 931–937.

Walker, R. M., Zhang, J., Chandra, Y., Dong, B. & Wang, Y. (2023). Revisiting the academic-practitioner divide: Evidence from computational social sciences and corpus linguistics. *Public administration review*, 83(6), 1599–1617.

Wang, Y. (2024). Does symbolic representation matter? A meta-analysis of the passive-symbolic representation link. *Public administration*, 83(6), 1599–1617. 10.1111/padm.12999.

Wu, X., He, Y.-L. & Sun, M. T.-W. (2013). Public administration research in mainland China and Taiwan: An assessment of journal publications, 1998–2008. *Public administration*, 91(2), 261–280.

Zhang, J., Chen, W., Petrovsky, N. & Walker, R. M. (2022). The expectation-disconfirmation model and citizen satisfaction with public services: A meta-analysis and an agenda for best practice. *Public administration review*, 82(1), 147–159.

Zhang, J., Li, H. & Yang, K. (2022). A meta-analysis of the government performance – trust link: Taking cultural and methodological factors into account. *Public administration review*, 82(1), 39–58.

Journals

Websites searched 15 December 2023 to collect information on journal aims and scope reported in the text.

Administration & Society: https://journals.sagepub.com/description/AAS

American Society for Public Administration: https://journals.sagepub.com/description/ARP

Environment and Planning C: Politics and Space: https://journals.sagepub.com/description/EPC

Governance: An International Journal of Policy, Administration and Institutions: https://onlinelibrary.wiley.com/journal/14680491

International Public Management Journal: www.tandfonline.com/action/journalInformation?show=aimsScope&journalCode=upmj20

International Review of Administrative Sciences: https://journals.sagepub.com/description/RAS

Journal of Public Administration Theory and Practice: https://academic.oup.com/jpart/pages/About

Local Government Studies: www.tandfonline.com/action/journalInformation?show=aimsScope&journalCode=flgs20

Public Administration: https://onlinelibrary.wiley.com/journal/14679299

Public Administration and Development: https://onlinelibrary.wiley.com/journal/1099162x

Public Administration Review: https://onlinelibrary.wiley.com/page/journal/ 15406210/homepage/productinformation.html

Public Management Review: www.tandfonline.com/action/journalInformation? show=aimsScope&journalCode=rpxm20

Public Money & Management: www.tandfonline.com/action/journalInforma tion?show=aimsScope&journalCode=rpmm20

Policy & Politics: https://onlinelibrary.wiley.com/journal/17471346

Public Performance and Management Review: www.tandfonline.com/action/ journalInformation?show=aimsScope&journalCode=mpmr20

Social Policy and Administration: https://onlinelibrary.wiley.com/journal/ 14679515

Acknowledgements

The authors would like to extend their deep gratitude to Claudia Avellaneda, Frances S. Berry, Maria Cuccinello, Bert George, Sharon Gilad, Ricardo Gomes, Soonhee Kim, Liang Ma, Janine O'Flynn, Rosemary O'Leary and Sandra van Thiel for freely offering their time and dedication and their deep disciplinary knowledge as members of the expert Delphi panel that named the fifty topics in public administration. Professional English language editing support provided by AsiaEdit (asiaedit.com).

Funding Statement

This work was supported by the University Grants Committee, Research Grants Council of Hong Kong (CityU 11601218).

Cambridge Elements ≡

Public and Nonprofit Administration

Andrew Whitford
University of Georgia

Andrew Whitford is Alexander M. Crenshaw Professor of Public Policy in the School of Public and International Affairs at the University of Georgia. His research centers on strategy and innovation in public policy and organization studies.

Robert Christensen
Brigham Young University

Robert Christensen is professor and George Romney Research Fellow in the Marriott School at Brigham Young University. His research focuses on prosocial and antisocial behaviors and attitudes in public and nonprofit organizations.

About the Series

The foundation of this series are cutting-edge contributions on emerging topics and definitive reviews of keystone topics in public and nonprofit administration, especially those that lack longer treatment in textbook or other formats. Among keystone topics of interest for scholars and practitioners of public and nonprofit administration, it covers public management, public budgeting and finance, nonprofit studies, and the interstitial space between the public and nonprofit sectors, along with theoretical and methodological contributions, including quantitative, qualitative and mixed-methods pieces.

The Public Management Research Association

The Public Management Research Association improves public governance by advancing research on public organizations, strengthening links among interdisciplinary scholars, and furthering professional and academic opportunities in public management.

Cambridge Elements ☰

Public and Nonprofit Administration

Elements in the Series

A full series listing is available at: www.cambridge.org/EPNP